DISASTER!

The Destruction of Our Planet

Other Scholastic paperbacks
you will enjoy:

Four Against the Odds:
The Struggle to Save Our Environment
by Stephen Krensky

Medical Mysteries:
Six Deadly Cases
by Dian Dincin Buchman

Our World of Mysteries
by Suzanne Lord

Volcanoes and Earthquakes
by Pat Lauber

Nobody Listens to Me
by Leslie Davis Guccione

DISASTER!

The Destruction of Our Planet

GEORGE SULLIVAN

SCHOLASTIC INC.
New York Toronto London Auckland Sydney

Photo Credits

Front cover courtesy of the USDA Forest Service. Pages 4, 7, 9, 13, 18, 25, 29, 31, 33, 56, 59, 61, 62, 64, 72, 74, 81, 83, 87, 89, 91, 97, 100, 104, 112, 114, 118, 126, 128, 130, 132 and 133 courtesy of AP/Wide World. Pages 15, 77, and 102 courtesy of George Sullivan. Page 19 courtesy of Ed Linton/U.S. Windpower. Page 32 courtesy of Eric Kroll. Page 39 courtesy of the National Park Service. Pages 41 and 49 courtesy of the U.S. Fish and Wildlife Service. Page 43 courtesy of the New York Zoological Society. Page 44 courtesy of The Rainforest Foundation. Pages 46, 52, 66, and 86 courtesy of UPI/Bettmann. Page 54 courtesy of The New York Post.

ISBN 0-590-44331-3

12 11 10 9 8 7 6 5 4 3 2   5 6 7/9

Printed in the U.S.A.   40

First Scholastic printing, December 1992

Contents

Introduction

Scientists predict the earth will probably last another 4 or 5 billion years. By that time, the sun will have burned so much of its own hydrogen fuel that it will expand to incinerate the planets, the earth included.

We may, however, be hastening the earth's passing by our own actions. This book describes some examples. Twenty people died and thousands were taken ill when factory smog blanketed a small Pennsylvania community. Deadly chemical wastes from industrial plants litter the landscape, causing entire towns to be abandoned. A meltdown and an explosion at a nuclear plant in what was once the Soviet Union spewed a deadly radioactive cloud over much of the planet.

The dictionary defines *warning* as something that makes us aware of possible trouble or danger. Within the past forty or so years, a variety of events have been warnings that we're seriously threatening life on the earth.

1
Death at Donora

Donora, Pennsylvania, is twenty-eight miles south of Pittsburgh and located on a U-shaped bend of the murky Monongahela River. It has hills on three sides that rise to about four hundred fifty feet. It is treeless and almost completely grassless. Its population today is around seventy-five hundred, but it used to be almost twice that.

Tuesday morning, October 26, 1948, dawned gray and cheerless in Donora. Thick fog and smoke had settled over the town. But most people paid no attention to it. The hills around Donora formed a natural hollow that had been filling with smoke since 1901. That year the town's two miles of waterfront had been taken over by the American Steel and Wire Company to use for a steel mill. Later the company added a plant where the wire was zinc-coated.

In 1948, in the main business section of Donora, low-hanging smog blotted out street lamps.

Because of the sheltering hills, no wind brushed away the smoke-laden mist. Sometimes the thick haze lasted two or three days. A few times it hung on as long as four days. The one that settled over Donora late in October, 1948, lasted six days. Not only was it the most persistent of Donora's smogs, it was also the deadliest.

Day by day, the stagnant air thickened. By Thursday afternoon, it was hardly possible to see across the street. The zinc mill, its tall stack still sending fumes into the air, had become no more than a blurry outline.

On Friday morning, about half of the town awoke coughing. Still, only a few people thought anything might be wrong. Autumn was always Donora's smokiest season. And, after all, it was

4

late in the fall, a time for bad colds. However, a group of miners who went to work that morning were surprised to find they were able to breathe more easily far down in the depths of the mine than they were at the surface.

One of the first people to realize that something serious was wrong was P. G. Hayes, the high school physics instructor. Mr. Hayes had asthma, a disease that makes breathing difficult and causes coughing. He had been told by his doctors that he must move out of the Donora area if he wanted to live. Instead, Mr. Hayes had equipped his home with an expensive electrostatic system that cleansed the air as it entered his house.

When Mr. Hayes left his home that Friday morning, he nearly choked to death. He quickly stumbled back inside. As soon as clean air filled his lungs, he was all right again.

Friday evening, many of the townspeople turned out for Donora's big Halloween parade, put on by the Chamber of Commerce each year. But the 1948 parade was unlike any that had gone before. All the children and many of the adults that lined the parade route had handkerchiefs tied over their noses and mouths to keep out the smoke. Even so, almost everyone was coughing. And the spectators could hardly see the marchers. They were like shadows going by.

The minute the parade was over, everybody hurried home to escape the fog. "In two minutes, there wasn't a soul left on the street," one resident recalled. "It was as quiet as midnight."

The smog claimed its first victim early Saturday morning. The man was elderly and had been sick for some time, so the death did not seem at all significant.

As he was dying, so were others. Between 2:00 A.M. and 4:00 P.M. on Saturday, fifteen people died. Ten died in five hours.

Somewhat typical was the death of John West. A perfectly healthy coal miner, Mr. West was walking home from work late Friday afternoon when he saw what he later described as a "big black cloud" heading in his direction. Frightened, West started to run for home. But the dark swirling mass swallowed him up. He gasped for breath as he staggered onward.

By the time he reached home, his head ached, his throat burned, and he had developed a dry, hacking cough. When his wife opened the door, Mr. West collapsed. "That black cloud is going to kill me," he told his wife.

John West was right. Two days later he died.

Hundreds of other people with the same symptoms fell ill Friday night and Saturday. One account of what happened says that about four thousand people were stricken.

Strangely, on Saturday morning, the community still did not realize it was in deep trouble. Everybody who was ill seemed to think that he or she was the only sick person in town. And many of those who were ill were elderly. This was normal, the people of Donora knew. The fog was always harder on the old than the young.

By October 30, 1948, the smog in Donora was so heavy that driving was nearly impossible and streets in the center of town were empty.

Besides, there was no one to tell the people of Donora that a disaster was in the making. There was no radio station in Donora and the television age was just dawning; few people had TV sets. Donora's only newspaper, the *Herald-American*, published only five days a week, Monday through Friday.

On Saturday, most of the townspeople went about their usual household tasks. That afternoon, when Donora and Monongahela high schools met in Donora for the traditional Smog Bowl football game, the stands were filled to capacity. Donora was heavily favored to win. But the team's star players were dazed and moved slowly. They seemed to be in a trance. Monongahela won easily, 26–7.

During the game, several spectators collapsed and had to be carried away. The public-address announcer kept reporting the names of people who were wanted at home "because of an emergency."

Donora had eight doctors. By Friday afternoon, their telephones were ringing constantly. Almost everyone had the same complaints — a splitting headache, choking and coughing, nausea and vomiting, and the inability to get their breath.

Dr. Ralph Koehler was one of Donora's doctors. His telephone kept ringing and ringing and the list of house visits he agreed to make kept getting longer and longer. "Something's coming off," Dr. Koehler told a colleague, "but I don't know what."

Dr. Edward Roth also realized "something was coming off." Many of the people he treated did not have asthma; nor had they ever displayed any kind of breathing trouble. The cause of what was taking place was no mystery to Dr. Roth. "It was obvious," he said, "that the smoke and the fog were to blame."

One of the biggest problems the doctors faced was getting from one patient to another. The fog was so thick it was nearly impossible to drive. Dr. Roth stopped trying. Instead, he made his rounds on foot.

Another problem was that he kept encountering other doctors. Some people, in their panic, called every doctor in town. Said Dr. Roth: "It was pretty discouraging to finally get someplace and drag

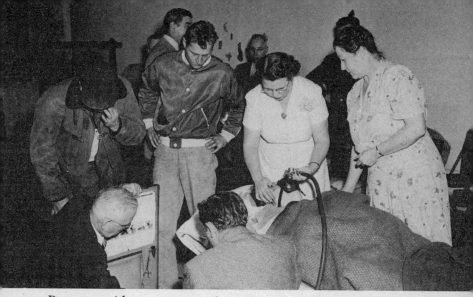

Donora residents overcome by smog were rushed to local hospitals.

yourself up the steps and be told that Dr. So-and-So had just been there."

The Donora Fire Department helped out, answering one emergency call after another — not fires, but people choking to death. Fireman Russ Davis responded to calls in his car, driving along the empty streets on the left side, with his head out the window, steering by scraping his left front tire against the curb.

When he arrived at the home of a victim, he found some people lying in bed, others lying on the floor. He covered each patient with a sheet or a blanket, then placed a cylinder of oxygen underneath it and opened the valve for fifteen minutes or so. "By, God, that rallied them!" he said.

The number of emergencies kept growing. One man came home from work and found his wife sitting on the edge of her bed gasping for breath, her head between her knees. The man fell asleep later that evening. When he awoke very early the next morning, his wife was dead, still sitting in the same position.

One woman was credited with saving her mother's life by getting her to breathe using a vacuum cleaner. The filter in the vacuum cleaner removed some of the impurities from the air as she inhaled.

The town's eight doctors worked steadily for over thirty-six hours. Donora's Red Cross director set up an emergency-aid station in the Community Center to take some of the pressure off of the doctors.

There were two hospitals in the area and they were soon overflowing with patients. In the Charleroi-Monessen hospital, six miles from Donora, the gasping, choking victims were placed in hallways when the beds became filled. "We can't take another patient," said Dr. James Lau, the hospital's superintendent. Oxygen tents were rushed to Donora from cities as far away as Cleveland.

Animals were stricken, too. Cats gasped and choked like humans. Dogs had runny eyes and noses. Cattle coughed. Canaries stopped singing and huddled in the bottom of their cages.

Radio broadcasts on Saturday night acquainted many townspeople with the seriousness of the situation. Some people reacted by fleeing the city.

On Sunday, the smoke-polluted air still clung to

Donora. But no one knew how many people were sick. The figure would not come out for several months. Most people thought it was only a few hundred. It was generally known that seventeen or eighteen people had died. By this time, the zinc plant had shut down, although the plant manager said he was sure that the mills had nothing to do with the problem.

Late on Sunday, it rained, washing the smog away. The townspeople could breathe again. Donora's ordeal had ended.

The six days of poisoned air had taken a heavy toll. Twenty residents of Donora had died. Of the town's 13,839 residents, 5,910 had become ill. Of these, 1,440 were listed as "seriously ill." A year later, some of them were still feeling the effects of what was called the "death smog."

The investigation of the catastrophe lasted almost a year. Conducted by the U.S. Public Health Service, it involved two-dozen specialists — chemists and engineers, meteorologists, physicians, and a veterinarian. They found a combination of factors had caused the disaster:

• Sulfur dioxide and other gases that poured from the many stacks in Donora and nearby communities.

• Tiny particles of iron oxide, zinc oxide, silicates, and carbon, all common substances in factory smoke.

• The weather. A condition known as an "inversion" existed over Donora at the time. The air near the ground, trapped by the surrounding hills, couldn't rise because it was colder than the air higher up. The layer of cold air lay on the hills like the lid on a kettle. Day by day, the polluted air stayed in the "kettle" until it became contaminated enough to kill.

Donora's nightmare marked a turning point in the health history of the United States. As Dr. Leonard A. Scheele, Surgeon General of the United States, put it, "Donora proved to us that smog no longer is just a nuisance — it is a menace to health." In the years that followed, the federal government spent millions of dollars investigating smog to make sure that what happened in Donora would not happen again.

Today, almost half a century after Donora, Americans still breathe dirty air. It's bad not only for people and animals, but for plants and trees as well.

The chief component of smog is *ozone*, a gas formed when nitrogen oxides and hydrocarbons are sent into the air from cars, trucks, and buses. Ozone also occurs naturally in the atmosphere, forming a thin shield that protects us from the sun's ultraviolet rays. But at ground level it's a health hazard. Industrial plants, electric utilities, and wood-burning stoves are offenders, too. Other sources, not as well known but just as hazardous, include the vapors given off by paints, dry-cleaning chemicals, and charcoal-lighting fuel.

Los Angeles is the nation's smog capital. During

*Cars on the Santa Monica Freeway in Los Angeles
whiz past a freeway condition sign that
bears a warning.*

the early 1990s, Los Angeles failed to meet air quality standards set by the federal government 160 to 175 days a year. That's about three times more than Houston, thirteen times more than New York, and twenty-five times more than Chicago.

But the air in Los Angeles is better than it used to be. Back in the late 1970s, Los Angeles was in violation of clean air standards nearly two hundred days a year.

Even some of the most isolated areas of the country don't escape. Sequoia and Kings Canyon National Parks, tucked away in the Sierra Nevada Mountains of eastern California, recorded even higher levels of ozone pollution in 1989 than many *cities*. During the summer of 1988, ozone levels were so high in Acadia National Park in Maine that officials were forced to issue their first health alert.

Sometimes you can smell polluted air and sometimes, when haze or smoke hangs in the air, you can see it. Whether you see it or not, air pollution can be dangerous. Even a little bit of it can cause your eyes to burn and your head to ache. It can tire you, blur your vision, and make it hard for you to breathe. Polluted air can make it easier for you to catch a cold or the flu. Air pollution has also been linked to such serious ailments as heart disease and cancer.

Researchers are also studying the harmful effects of *acid rain*, the popular term used for rain, snow, sleet, or other precipitation that has been polluted by sulfur oxides or nitrogen oxides, forming sulfuric acids and nitric acids. When these chemical compounds fall back to earth as rain, they cause great damage to lakes, rivers, and streams, killing fish and other aquatic life.

The deadly process starts at the very bottom of the food chain. Acid in the water destroys the life forms on which minnows and other small fish feed. It kills young fish and harms older fish by attacking their gills and interfering with oxygen circulation. In extreme cases, entire lakes become lifeless.

In Canada, one hundred fifty thousand eastern lakes — one out of every seven — have already been damaged by acid rain. In the United States,

Decades of exposure to polluted air ravaged the copper skin of the Statue of Liberty.

lakes in fourteen eastern states have acid levels high enough to harm fish.

Acid rain also causes a buildup of poisonous materials in soil. This weakens trees, making them more likely to fall victim to disease and drought, sometimes causing whole forests to be wiped out.

In addition to living things, tens of thousands of historic buildings and monuments are at risk from acid rain, which damages marble and limestone and causes metal alloys to corrode more rapidly. A study by the Environmental Protection Agency (EPA) estimates that acid rain has defaced buildings in seventeen states east of the Mississippi River. The United States Capitol and the Washington Monument are among those struc-

15

tures that have been scarred. The corrosion of the copper exterior of the Statue of Liberty was one of the chief reasons that the monument was closed down for a two-year "facelift" during the mid-1980s. Steel components in bridges are being corroded, as is the nation's fleet of B–52 bombers, a problem that costs the Air Force millions of dollars a year.

In the United States, people have been fighting air pollution for decades, and their efforts are showing results. For example, many factories and utilities must now control pollutants discharged into the air, which are emissions, with "scrubbers" — equipment that removes sulfur oxides from gases produced when coal is burned.

Automobiles are now equipped with a device called a "catalytic converter." It changes the harmful hydrocarbons and carbon monoxide a car normally produces into harmless carbon dioxide and water. Since a car with a catalytic converter uses unleaded gas, converters have also helped to reduce lead levels in the air.

Thanks in a large part to emission controls, the air we breathe today is better than it used to be. But there is still a long way to go. Late in 1990, the EPA revealed that 130 million Americans live in areas that do not comply with federal smog clean-air standards.

The 1990 Clean Air Act will help. Cities must conform to specific clean-air standards within strict time limits. Auto companies must produce cars with improved emissions-control standards. Small businesses — responsible for hundreds of tons of pollution a year — are going to have to clean up their acts.

The air quality would be better if the nation were not so dependent on oil. Environmentalists believe that the United States should commit itself toward cutting its consumption of oil. A 50-percent reduction in oil use by the year 2000 is one suggested goal.

A similar policy is needed concerning the use of coal, the chief producer of greenhouse gases and acid rain, and a major factor in the formation of smog. One recommendation calls for a 50-percent reduction in the use of coal by 2020.

To those who say such reductions are too drastic, environmentalists point to the notable energy savings produced in the 1970s, during the presidential terms of Richard Nixon, Gerald Ford, and especially Jimmy Carter. Government regulations doubled the mileage of new American cars. New standards regarding home insulation forced down the consumption of energy.

Also during the 1970s, the government encouraged the development of energy-saving technologies and alternative fuels. One example: the electric car. Powered by batteries, which produce no exhaust, electric cars have been in the planning stages for years. It may soon be possible to mass-produce them.

When it comes to alternative fuels, one of the simplest is solar energy, specifically "passive" solar

This house has solar collectors facing south and an overhang that provides shade from the summer sun yet lets in the low winter sun.

energy. This often involves designing a home or an office building so that its windows face mainly toward the sun so they are able to harvest the maximum amount of the sun's light and heat. Solar panels on the roof supply all or most of the building's hot-water needs.

Such buildings are already a reality. By the early 1990s, in fact, more than one million American homes had been designed and built to take advantage of passive solar energy.

The most promising invention of the last twenty years, according to Michael Oppenheimer of the Environmental Defense Fund, is the photovoltaic cell, which turns the sun's radiant energy into electricity. By the mid-1990s, some utility companies

At Altamont Pass, California, these wind turbines generate power for the Pacific Gas and Electric Company.

may find solar cells cheaper than coal or oil for particular power needs.

Wind power represents another alternative energy source. Like solar power, energy derived from the wind is safe and secure, clean and cheap. And no matter how much we use, we'll never run out.

There are a couple of contributions you can make. Whenever you want to go someplace, try not to rely on a car. Perhaps you can walk or ride a bike. The less your family uses a car, the cleaner the air will be.

You can also help by getting your parents to switch from standard light bulbs to energy-efficient compact fluorescents, which use anywhere from 65 percent to 75 percent less electricity than regular bulbs.

One quality that many air pollutants have is that they're invisible. This makes the problems they cause more difficult to solve. When the catastrophe occurred at Donora, Pennsylvania, in 1948, the pollution took the form of thick black smoke. It burned people's eyes and seared their lungs. And you could see it. People fled in horror to escape it.

But when air pollutants stream out of the tailpipe of your family's car or are sent up industrial chimneys or stacks, they often can't be seen. But those invisible gases are capable of doing as much damage to the planet as the blackest of polluting clouds.

2
Buried Bombshells

Motorists traveling Interstate 44 just west of St. Louis, Missouri, come to a stretch where the highway signs have been painted over, blotting out the name that once appeared. To the north of the highway, weeds and tall grass conceal what used to be a town. There are streets, rusting mobile homes, and tumbledown houses with broken windows resting on cement-block foundations.

You can see the hulks of rotting cars, TV sets, red wagons, and discarded furniture. Hand-painted signs reflect a grim humor, painted on front doors or the sides of houses. SEND HELP, says one. GONE AND FORGOTTEN, declares another.

The 7-Eleven is boarded up. So is Adams' Donut and Coffee Shop. Everything is gray and dirty. There are no people.

This is Times Beach, Missouri, a town that has

been declared legally dead. Not long before Christmas in 1982, the federal government announced that the streets of Times Beach had been soaked with dioxin, one of the most toxic substances in the world.

Dioxin is used in manufacturing some weed and insect killers. It was one of the ingredients in Agent Orange, the defoliant used extensively in Vietnam during the Vietnam War.

Dioxin appears to be the most powerful cancer-causing agent ever tested in laboratory rodents. It is so powerful that two drops in ten thousand gallons of water is considered a dangerous concentration.

Even before its encounter with dioxin, Times Beach was unusual. It was created in the 1920s by a newspaper, *The St. Louis Times*. By buying a six-month subscription and paying another $67.50, you could get a plot of land that measured 20 by 100 feet along the Meramec River about twenty-five miles west of St. Louis.

At first Times Beach was a summer community. But little by little it changed into a working-class town of permanent residents who lived in small clapboard houses or trailer homes.

It never grew larger than one square mile. It never grew large enough to be included on even the most detailed maps of Missouri.

One problem with Times Beach was that it was located on a flood plain. The Meramec River overflowed occasionally, but Times Beach residents, many of whom like to refer to themselves as River

Rats, took the flooding in stride. They were an independent bunch. In fact, when the federal government told the people of Times Beach to build their homes according to certain regulations or lose their flood insurance, they ignored the warning. "They just did not want the federal government telling them what to do," one official recalls.

Another problem for Times Beach was dust. Along the town's ten miles or so of unpaved roads, pickup trucks, motorcycles, and other vehicles kicked up thick clouds of limestone dust that choked the countryside.

To control the dust, the town called Russell Bliss. That was in May 1971. It was the most fateful call in Times Beach history.

Russell Bliss earned his living as a hauler of industrial wastes. Driving his truck through rural communities in eastern Missouri, Bliss was hired to spray waste oil on dirt roads, parking lots, and the floors of horse barns to keep down the dust.

In May 1971, Bliss sprayed oil at Judy Piatt's stables near Moscow Mills, Missouri. Within a few days, hundreds of birds nesting in the stable's rafters fell to the ground and died. In the weeks that followed, more than twenty of her cats went bald and died. And over the next three-and-a-half years, sixty-two horses owned by Ms. Piatt also died.

Ms. Piatt started having headaches and chest pains. She also suffered from diarrhea. And one of her daughters started hemorrhaging.

By 1974, investigators representing the Centers for Disease Control in Atlanta identified dioxin as the poison that had contaminated Ms. Piatt's horse barn and other sites throughout eastern Missouri.

The chemical had been produced by the Northeastern Pharmaceutical and Chemical Company in Verona, Missouri. This was the first link in a long chain of events that caused the ordeal of Times Beach.

When Northeastern Pharmaceutical and Chemical went out of business in 1971, the company hired one of its suppliers, Independent Petrochemical Corporation of St. Louis, to dispose of its chemical wastes. To do the job, Independent Petrochemical turned to — you guessed it — Russell Bliss.

For at least two summers during the early 1970s, Bliss sprayed tens of thousands of gallons of waste sludge from Independent Petrochemical all over Times Beach. Michael Reid, who used to live there, remembers that he and other kids loved to bicycle behind Mr. Bliss's truck, skidding and sliding in the thick oil.

"I remember riding our bikes through it," says Yolanda Bohrer, a long-time resident of Times Beach, "and getting all dirty and tracking it into the house and getting into trouble." When residents tried to hose off the oil that had splashed onto their cars, Ms. Bohrer recalls, they removed the car paint as well.

During this period, the problem of dioxin-contaminated soil was still not considered serious. It was believed that the chemicals would remain

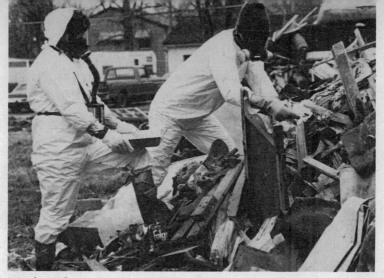

Workers from the Environmental Protection Agency take samples of debris in Times Beach, Missouri, after flood waters had receded.

toxic for only six months or so — a deadly miscalculation.

Rumors that many sites in eastern Missouri had been contaminated with oil containing dioxin began spreading during the mid-1970s. The Environmental Protection Agency (EPA) eventually prepared a list of the sites. The names of thirty towns and cities were on the list. Times Beach was one of them.

Late in November 1982, the EPA went into Times Beach to test soil samples. One test site was on property owned by LaVerne "Skip" Baker and her husband. The Bakers had bought a one bedroom home in Times Beach in 1955 and, over the years, had added four more rooms. There they brought up their seven children.

One November morning in 1982, Mrs. Baker found men in silvery white jumpsuits drilling holes in the ground near her house. "I was getting ready to go to work," she recalled, "and I saw these men running around with masks on."

Before the EPA could analyze the soil and announce the results of the tests, the Bakers and everyone else in Times Beach were struck another blow. The waters of the Meramec River swept through the town in what was the worst flood in Times Beach's history. Virtually every one of the town's eight hundred dwellings was damaged or destroyed.

"This is phenomenal," said Fred A. Lafser, director of the Missouri Department of Natural Resources. "Very few people in the world have dioxin problems and very few people in the world have flood problems. We have both."

Two days before Christmas, the EPA released the agency's test results. They confirmed the worst fears of residents — that dangerous concentrations of dioxin were in the soil.

At a town meeting with federal and state health officials, Dr. Henry Falk, representing the Centers for Disease Control, told the people who had left Times Beach after the flooding to stay away. He told those who had returned to avoid exposure to soil and debris.

According to Dr. Falk, scientific studies with animals indicated that dioxin can be dangerous to the skin, the liver, and the immune system. Many of the townspeople attending the meeting told Dr. Falk of persistent rashes and other ills, all perhaps related to dioxin pollution.

The Baker family was one with serious health problems. "I've got one granddaugher that's got leukemia," Mrs. Baker said. "My one daughter lost a baby. It deteriorated in the womb and she's never been able to get pregnant again."

Marilyn Leistner, the town's mayor, had four children, all in their twenties. "One of my daughters has a serious disorder," she said. "Another had an operation for cancer of the cervix at twenty-one."

Said Dr. Falk: "It would be difficult to overstate the problem here."

When EPA scientists took more soil samples and found dioxin present in many streets and roadside ditches, residents questioned whether there was any danger, even after the flood. "I've lived here thirty years and built a good life here," said Evelyn Zufall. "I can't believe this is as dangerous as they tell us."

Mrs. Zufall's children were among those who rode their bikes behind Russell Bliss's spray truck. "They did not get sick," she said. "Nor did anyone else I know."

Gary Stein, also from the Centers for Disease Control, had an answer for Mrs. Zufall and the others who had voiced doubts about leaving Times Beach. He compared them to long-term smokers who had no apparent ill effects from it yet. His advice to them would be to quit smoking. To the residents of Times Beach, he said, "Leave your homes — now."

While the EPA was spreading the word about the hazards of Times Beach, the state of Missouri was holding hearings on the dioxin situation. Russell Bliss was called upon to testify. "I swear to all of you," Bliss said, choking back tears, "I had no idea this dioxin-contaminated oil was bad — as God is my witness."

Mr. Bliss paused for a few seconds and then added, "I just wish this oil had been disposed of in some other way."

Early in 1983, the federal government announced it would spend almost $35 million to buy up all the homes in Times Beach and help the people get settled elsewhere. Most of the residents greeted the announcement with a sense of relief. Some complained, however, that they were not being paid enough for their homes.

Almost all residents seemed sad to leave. "I've been here twenty-three years," said sixty-three-year-old J. D. Lindley, "and everything we have is here. But I'm ready for the buyout now."

Everybody eventually left Times Beach, except one couple, George Klein, seventy-one years old, and his wife, Ida Lorene, sixty-one years old. Married for forty-three years, the Kleins had always lived in the same white house, tending their garden and raspberry and blackberry bushes. They had no dioxin fears. "The way I feel," said Mr. Klein, "is that if they let it go for ten years and they let

During a press conference, children in Times Beach, Missouri, wait to hear what the federal government planned to do to help them.

you live here, what harm can it do you? If it hasn't got you yet, it won't bother you now."

Only one road linked the Kleins and Times Beach with the outside world, and that was straddled by a checkpoint manned by armed security guards. Their job was to turn away sightseers. To visit the Kleins, friends and relatives were asked to wear disposable jumpsuits provided by the guards. The Kleins said they had no neighbors before the evacuation, so it didn't bother them that they had none after it.

The final scene in the drama of Times Beach was written when the town's Board of Aldermen voted to disincorporate the city. Technically, Times Beach no longer existed.

* * *

Times Beach isn't in the headlines any more. But similar toxic wastes menace cities and towns across the United States. Hazardous wastes not only pollute the land, they also pollute waters underneath or next to the land.

Waste materials are classified as hazardous when they are poisonous, inflammable or explosive, corrosive, or are able to react with other chemicals. Every year, some 250 million tons of hazardous wastes are produced in the United States.

For years, companies disposed of hazardous wastes by either dumping them or burying them in the land. People did not realize how dangerous they were or, if they did realize it, they failed to do anything.

Take, for instance, a neighborhood in Niagara Falls, New York, known as Love Canal. The neighborhood got its name from an abandoned canal into which the Hooker Chemicals and Plastics Company dumped thousands of containers filled with toxic chemicals for more than ten years.

The poisons seeped into the backyards and basements of nearby homes, creating hazardous vapors. Residents experienced extremely high rates of illness, cancer, birth defects, and miscarriages. By 1978, Love Canal had become a national symbol of the deadly dangers of toxic-waste dumping. President Jimmy Carter declared a national health emergency for the area. More than two thousand people left their homes, turning Love Canal into a boarded up ghost town.

A child endangered by the Love Canal chemicals waves a protest banner at a neighborhood meeting in August, 1978.

In the years following the Love Canal disaster, investigators uncovered more and more lethal dump sites. Nearly every section of North America had its own trouble spot:

• In New Jersey, officials ordered a landfill in Ocean County to be closed after toxic chemicals, including some that cause cancer, were found contaminating nearby wells.

• Dioxin was found leaking from dozens of metal drums found buried near a farm not far from Aurora, Missouri. EPA officials believed that the chemical wastes in the drums had come from a local pharmaceutical plant.

• Water wells in Toone, Tennessee, were found to have been contaminated by pesticide wastes

A cat in an animal reserve in Ontario, Canada, that became sick after eating contaminated fish.

leaking from three hundred thousand 55-gallon drums.

• Vinyl chloride was found to be leaking from a municipal landfill in the Long Island town of Islip, New York. Nearby wells had to be closed, a school was shut down, and four houses condemned.

In 1980, to cope with the health problems linked to hazardous waste dump-sites, the federal government passed the Comprehensive Environmental Response, Compensation, and Liability Act. Known popularly as the "Superfund," it provided $1.6 billion to clean up some two thousand unsafe dump sites. An estimated fourteen thousand additional sites that were considered potential haz-

Workers open some of the more than 10,000 drums filled with chemicals at a hazardous waste site in Hamilton, Ohio, in 1982.

33

ards would be monitored. A 1986 act provided an additional $9 billion.

Hazardous wastes are not merely the result of industrial processes in factories or laboratories — not by any means. Suppose that an attendant at a gasoline station, in filling the tank of your parents' car, spills some on the ground. That spilled gasoline is a "hazardous waste."

Many products used daily in our homes contain hazardous substances. These include polishes and cleansers, disinfectants and glues, and paints and paint thinners. When such substances are poured down a drain or tossed into a garbage bag, they can end up seeping from landfills into water and soil.

Household batteries — the type used to power toys, radios, tools, and many small appliances used in the home, and that are sold by the billions — can be a serious environmental hazard. Batteries contain toxic metals, and when the batteries are dumped, these metals can leak into the ground. If the batteries are burned, the toxic metals escape as air pollutants.

From an environmental point of view, rechargeable batteries are better to use than regular alkaline batteries. When one runs down, you put it into a recharger, which is plugged into a wall socket. The recharger draws electricity from the outlet and re-energizes the battery. Because a battery of this type can be recharged more than a hundred times, you use much fewer of them.

In Japan, garbage managers require that household batteries be collected separately from other wastes, in order to dispose of them safely. Eleven European countries also have battery-collection programs. But the United States lags behind other nations in dealing with waste batteries and the environmental damage they cause. As of 1991, only a handful of American communities had battery-collection programs.

Flea collars are another common source of toxic chemicals. They contain pesticides that can actually be harmful to your pet, and are a potential threat to the environment when tossed away. Instead of flea collars, try this alternative: Process orange or grapefruit skins in a food blender. Simmer the paste with some water. After the mixture has cooled, brush it onto your pet's fur.

"Vast quantities of detergents, bleaches, and polishes are manufactured from toxic chemicals like hydrochloric acid, sulfuric acid, and benzene," says Diane MacEachern, author of *Save the Planet, 750 Everyday Ways You Can Help Clean Up the Earth*. "Just disposing of the 'empty' containers these chemicals come in can send them right to the landfill, where the toxins leach into the groundwater — possibly to end up back in the kitchen, coming out the tap."

Toxic-free cleansers can be made from simple household items like vinegar, ammonia, borax, and baking soda. Using these instead of detergents, bleaches, and polishes made from toxic chemicals is a means of pollution prevention. Environmentalists urge manufacturers using toxic chemicals to consider changing raw materials from toxic to nontoxic. Says noted environmentalist Barry Commoner: "The best way to stop toxic chemicals from entering the environment is not to use them."

3
Vanishing Wildlife

If present trends continue, the giant panda could become extinct within the next century. That's the opinion of scientists who have studied this fascinating bearlike animal with woolly fur and distinctive black and white markings.

According to official statistics released by the government of China (pandas live high in the mountains of southwest China), there are about one thousand pandas left in the wild. The previous panda census, taken in the late 1970s, counted about twice that number. Another one hundred pandas live in zoos and breeding centers.

There are two major threats to the giant panda: hunting, and the loss of its living places, or habitat.

Hunting, or poaching, is the most serious problem. Hunters kill pandas for their pelts. A panda pelt — the skin with the fur still on it — can bring as much as $20,000 in some parts of China.

Although the Chinese government has established the death penalty for poaching and trading in panda pelts, and four hunters have been sentenced to death, the problem has not been solved. "If poaching isn't checked, the panda will disappear," says George Schaller, a noted conservationist.

The other problem involves the panda's diet. Pandas live mainly on bamboo shoots, stems, and leaves. An adult panda consumes about forty pounds of bamboo each day.

Pandas live where bamboo grows, at elevations of 6,000 to 12,000 feet. But in China, where wood and land that can support farming is scarce, local residents have cut down huge areas of bamboo forests. That means that pandas are no longer able to roam freely in search of food, water, and shelter.

Some experts say that the panda's best chance of survival comes from zoos, protected reserves, and breeding centers. But institutions that control pandas have had only limited success in raising them. For example, in twenty years of panda breeding in China, only twenty-eight pandas have been bred and raised successfully in captivity.

"We know the panda must rely on man to survive," Pan Wenshi, a panda specialist at China's Beijing University, told *The New York Times* in 1991. "But man has not yet offered a good way of helping it."

Wildlife species are becoming extinct at a rapid

The grizzly bear is an endangered species, which means they are likely to become extinct if not protected.

rate. It's almost as if humanity is at war with the animals and plants with whom we share the planet. In North America alone, some six hundred animals and plants are now classified as endangered or threatened. Worldwide, the number reaches well into the thousands. "Endangered" species are those that, under the terms of the federal Endangered Species Act, seem likely to become extinct if not protected. "Threatened" species are those likely to become endangered within the foreseeable future. The two terms apply to plants as well as animals.

Some endangered animals are well-known: besides the giant panda, there's the leopard, Asian elephant, black rhinoceros, grizzly bear, and West Indian manatee.

Some Endangered Mammals and Birds in the World

Mammals — Range

Asian wild ass — Southwestern and central Asia
Bobcat — Central Mexico
Cheetah — Africa to India
Asian elephant — Southeastern and central Asia
Chinese river dolphin — China
Bactrian camel — Mongolia, China
Gorilla — Central and Western Africa
Leopard — Africa, Asia
Asiatic lion — Turkey to India
Howler monkey — Mexico to South America
Giant panda — China
Black rhinoceros — Sub-Saharan Africa
Tiger — Asia
Gray whale — North Pacific Ocean
Wild yak — Tibet, India
Mountain zebra — South Africa

Birds — Range

Hooded crane — Japan, Russia
Indigo macaw — Brazil
West African ostrich — Spanish Sahara
Golden parakeet — Brazil
Australian parrot — Australia

Others are not. In fact, thousands of species that scientists forecast will be extinct by the year 2000 have never even been identified. Biologist David Janzen of the University of Pennsylvania describes that catastrophe in these terms: "It's as though the

The American bald eagle, a symbol of the United States, is an endangered species.

nations of the world decided to burn their libraries without bothering to see what was in them."

If just one species disappears, many others suffer. It's like losing "strands in the web of life," says John Fitzgerald of Defenders of Wildlife. This is because animal and plant species interact in delicately balanced ecosystems. For example, insects are eaten by shrews (small mouselike animals with sharp snouts) and shrews are eaten by owls. If owls should become scarce, the animals they eat increase in number and become pests.

Another example: If people kill too many snakes and lizards, the mice that the snakes and lizards eat multiply and begin to consume farmers' crops.

Although most news stories about endangered species focus on animals, plants are in just as much trouble. The Center for Plant Conservation has predicted that 680 existing plant types in the United States alone could disappear during the 1990s — over three times the number lost during the previous two centuries.

Hawaii alone accounts for more than one fourth of the nation's endangered plant species. One half of Hawaii's twenty-four hundred plant species are considered threatened.

Hawaii's forest system is the eighth largest in the United States, although Hawaii has only 0.2 percent of the nation's land area, and it faces a unique menace. Wild pigs, goats, and cattle have uprooted or trampled the forest's native vegetation.

When plant species are wiped out, serious problems for the global community occur. Plants, first of all, are food for both humans and meat-producing animals. They also provide timber, fibers, latex, gums, oils, resins, fats, and waxes.

As plant species disappear, we end up losing life-saving medicines. About 25 percent of the pharmaceuticals in use today contain ingredients that originally came from wild plants. An endangered species of evening primrose provides medicine for the treatment of heart disease and arthritis. The rosy periwinkle, a rare plant from the island of Madagascar, provides the cure for a type of childhood leukemia. The plant was found, fortunately, before its native habitat was destroyed.

In the past, animal and plant species died out

An animal graveyard erected for Earth Day at New York's Bronx Zoo has more than 200 white tombstones for animals that are extinct.

as a result of natural causes. Some, for example, perished because of changes in the earth's climate.

Nowadays, however, wildlife species become extinct because of humans. The problem involves *habitats* — living places that provide each species with food and water and whatever else it needs for survival. Each species is suited to its own habitat and usually cannot live anywhere else. Humans, in their never-ending search for farmland, living space, wood, and minerals, have destroyed countless wildlife habitats.

Much of this destruction is taking place in the tropical rain forests of the world. Occupying about 7 percent of the earth's land surface, the tropical rain forests are located between the Tropic of Ca-

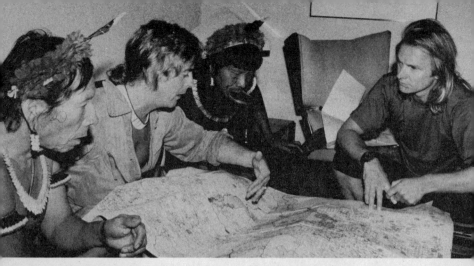

The Rainforest Foundation works with inhabitants of the South American rainforest and rock musician Sting to draw attention to the disappearing rainforest.

pricorn and Tropic of Cancer, the lines of latitude that embrace the Equator and the globe's Torrid Zone.

While the areas covered by the rain forests are relatively small, they are believed to contain between 50 and 75 percent of the planet's animal and plant species. And most of these cannot be found elsewhere. For example, six square miles of healthy forest in Massachusetts or Minnesota, or about anywhere else in the world where the climate might be called *temperate*, contain about forty plant species. Scientists who studied the same amount of land in a Malaysian rain forest identified *320,000* individual plants, representing *835* species.

There are countless examples of the abundant

animal species in the rain forest. In 1989, in Peru's Tambopata Reserve, biologist Edward Wilson found forty-three different ant species on *a single tree*. Ninety percent of all monkeys and apes are found in the tropical forest regions of Asia, Africa, and Latin America.

Now these rain forests are under attack. In Brazil, the lush forests south of the Amazon River are being slashed and burned to establish cattle ranches to provide more steaks and hamburger. Brazilians are also growing sugar cane — not for food — but to make *gasahol*, a mixture of alcohol (made from sugar) and gasoline that is used to fuel cars and trucks.

In Africa, Indonesia, and Malayasia, forest growth is being replaced with plantations that grow bananas, oil palms, and rubber.

The rate of destruction has been estimated at one acre *per second*. Each year, this amounts to a chunk of land roughly the size of Wyoming.

One hopeful sign from recent scientific studies shows that simply leaving forests alone is sometimes more profitable than clearing them. According to these reports, harvesting products such as rubber and fiber from a healthy forest can provide more income than clearing vast areas for timber or cattle pasture. Environmental groups are seeking to convince governments that proper forest-management has benefits.

The problems involved in preserving tropical rain forests and their wildlife habitats are very

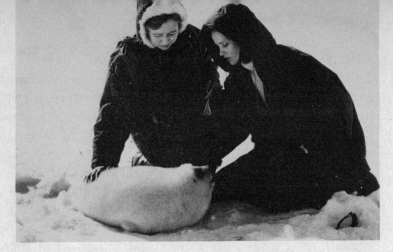

Members of a group known as Beauty Without Cruelty, which opposes the killing of seals, kneel with a two-week-old harp seal pup. A few minutes after this photo was taken, the pup was clubbed and skinned.

complicated. But one way you can help is by joining an international wildlife protection group. The most noted is the World Wildlife Fund located in Washington, DC.

This organization is well-known for its campaigns to save certain animals, such as the panda (which is its emblem) and Asia's Bengal tiger. The World Wildlife Fund also helped to stop the slaughter of Africa's mountain gorilla and the Latin American jaguar.

During the mid-1980s, the World Wildlife Fund launched its "Plant Campaign" meant to make people aware of the destruction of plant species and to suggest some solutions to the problem. "Saving the Plants That Save" is the campaign's slogan.

Some Endangered Mammals in North America

Mammals — Range

Ozark big-eared bat — Missouri, Oklahoma, Arizona
Brown and Grizzly bear — Most of the United States
Eastern cougar — Eastern North America
Columbian white-tailed deer — Washington, Oregon
San Joaquin kit-fox — California
Southeastern beach mouse — Florida
Ocelot — Texas, Arizona
Southern sea otter — Washington, Oregon, California
Florida panther — Louisiana, Arkansas; east to South
  Carolina, Florida
Utah prairie dog — Utah
Morro Bay kangaroo rat — California
Carolina northern flying squirrel — North Carolina,
  Tennessee
Red wolf — Southeast to Central Texas

In your own community, you may be able to play an active role by volunteering at a fish or wildlife refuge. You might be able to help out at the visitor's center or give tours. There are often a wide variety of wildlife management chores to be performed. These include banding wildlife, doing bird counts, and building shelters and nesting structures.

Since 1620, the year the Pilgrims landed on Plymouth Rock in Massachusetts, native plants and animals have been under attack. Scientists

Some Endangered Birds, Reptiles, and Fish in North America

Birds — Range

Masked bobwhite (quail) — Arizona
California condor — Oregon, California
Whooping crane — Rocky Mountains east to the
   Carolinas, Canada
Eskimo curlew — Alaska and North Canada
Bald eagle — Most of the United States and Canada
American peregrine falcon — Canada to Mexico
Hawaiian hawk — Hawaii
Attwater's greater prairie chicken — Texas
Bachman's warbler (wood) — Southeastern North
   America, Cuba
Kirtland's warbler (wood) — Most of the United
   States, Canada, the Bahama Islands
Ivory-billed woodpecker — Southeast, South Central
   States, Cuba

Reptiles — Range

American alligator — Southeast
American crocodile — Florida
Atlantic salt-marsh snake — Florida
Plymouth red-bellied turtle — Massachusetts

Fish — Range

Yaqui catfish — Arizona
Bonytail chub — Arizona, California, Colorado,
   Nevada, Utah, Wyoming

Since 1969, when selling alligator skins became illegal, the alligator population has increased from a few hundred thousand to several million.

estimate that habitat destruction has caused the permanent loss of some five hundred wildlife species in North America.

But there have been some success stories. During the mid-1960s, the American alligator was classified as endangered due to overhunting. But thanks to the efforts of conservationists, the alligator has been reclassified as merely threatened. Following the ban on the pesticide DDT in 1972, the brown pelican and bald eagle populations have increased.

There is cause for hope. By working together, we can help to turn the tide of destruction that threatens the planet.

4
The Biggest Threat

GLOBAL FOOD CRISIS WORSENS

GREAT PLAINS DROUGHT IN SEVENTH YEAR

TROPICAL DISEASES SPREADING IN SOUTHERN U.S.

MAYOR OF CHARLESTON DECLARES
HEALTH EMERGENCY AS FLOOD
WATERS CONTINUE TO RISE

KEY WEST DROWNS

Within the next fifty years or so, many scientists believe that these may be typical headlines. About one half the people alive today might read them someday.

Scorching temperatures, long droughts, severe floods — these could all result from global warming. Probably no greater threat menaces the world today, say environmentalists.

Global warming results from the "greenhouse effect." The earth is surrounded by a blanket of invisible gases, chiefly carbon dioxide, methane, nitrous oxide, and chloroflurocarbons (CFCs). These gases play much the same role as the glass panes in a greenhouse. They let in the warming rays of the sun but keep excess heat from radiating back into space. If it were not for the greenhouse gases, the world would be so cold humans could not survive.

But carbon dioxide and other industrial gases are being produced in such enormous quantities that they're thickening the greenhouse "blanket." More and more of the sun's heat is being trapped as a result.

If this trend continues, the results could be disastrous by around the year 2035. The polar ice caps could melt, raising sea levels around the world and flooding coastal areas. Residents of New York and San Francisco might find themselves underwater. Half of Florida and Louisiana would disappear. So would sizeable chunks of Virginia and Delaware. The waters of San Francisco Bay would flood the Sacramento Valley.

The Potomac and Anacostia rivers would rise to cover much of Washington, DC. If Congress persisted in convening at the Capitol, which, fortunately, perches atop Capitol Hill, they could do so, but members would have to arrive by boat.

On a 101° day, this young boy cooled off in the shadow of the United Nations in New York City.

Were the sea level to rise fifteen feet or so, enormous tracts of farmland in the Netherlands, Bangladesh, Thailand, Vietnam, Kampuchea, and China would vanish.

Thirteen million citizens of Bangladesh live on land that is less than ten feet above sea level. Their country is already one of the rainiest in the world. Should the waters of the Bay of Bengal start to rise because of the melting ice caps, what would happen to the Bangladeshis?

Global warming would also cause most of the world to experience hot days, and the hottest days would be hotter than they are now. Take Washington, DC, for instance. The city now experiences one 100° day a year, on average. Climatologist Jim Hansen of NASA's Goddard Institute for Space

Studies figured out that, should the output of carbon dioxide double, the temperature there would soar above 100° twelve days a year. Eighty-seven days would have temperatures above 90° — as opposed to thirty-six days now.

In most parts of the world, winters would be warmer and wetter; summers, hotter and drier. The Sahara may become hotter than anyplace on earth has ever been in history.

The tropics would suffer the most. Dry areas would become drier. Humid areas would experience more rainfall.

It wouldn't be bad in every part of the world, however. The northernmost areas, including parts of Russia, Canada, Alaska, Scandinavia, and Japan might even benefit. Soil-rich portions of Canada and Russia, where the growing season is now too short for them to be productive, might rival Iowa and Nebraska in agricultural output. Through an increase in its grazing land, sheep production in Iceland might double.

The increase in temperature would also disrupt the circulation patterns of the oceans. For example, the Gulf Stream might grow weaker. As it is now, the Gulf Stream's flow is powered by the difference in temperatures between the Equator and the poles. The ocean acts as a pump, redistributing solar heat. "If the earth warms," says Bill Jenkins, an oceanographer at the Woods Hole (Massachusetts) Oceanographic Institute, "the poles might get hotter, reducing the thermal contrast and reducing the strength of the pump."

A weakening of the Gulf Stream could create cooler temperatures in the coastal areas of the Carolinas, Virginia, and Maryland. Great Britain credits its relatively mild winter temperatures to the Gulf Stream. Winters there could get chillier.

What's scary about all of this is that temperature statistics indicate that global warming has already started to happen. All of the hottest years on record occurred quite recently. Since record-keeping began in 1896, the hottest year was 1990, according to American and British scientists. The next hottest year was 1991. In descending order, the seven warmest years on record are as follows: 1990, 1991, 1988, 1983, 1987, 1944, and 1989.

The study was done by NASA's Goddard Institute for Space Studies in New York City and the

During the summer of 1991, the northeastern United States suffered its worst heat wave in years.

British Meterological Office. They used a multitude of thermometers on land and at sea. According to the study, the warmer weather was most apparent over the United States and southern Canada, Europe, western Siberia, and the Far East.

While scientists have had no trouble establishing that the earth is warming up, they're not quite ready to say *why* it is. It could be the greenhouse effect; it could also be caused by some natural phenomenon, one not yet completely understood.

More and more scientists are coming to believe that global warming is caused by greenhouse gases such as carbon dioxide. "I've been skeptical about saying it's an enhanced greenhouse effect," says Jim Angell, a climate expert at the National Oceanic and Atmospheric Administration's Air Resources Laboratory in Silver Spring, Maryland. "But it's getting harder to defend that skepticism."

What can be done to slow the pace of global warming? The basic problem is carbon dioxide, which accounts for about one half of the greenhouse gases. Factories and electric power plants that burn coal or oil — fossil fuels — are the worst offenders. Through conservation and energy efficiency, we must put the brakes on the burning of fossil fuels.

A second solution is simple: plant a tree. One growing tree consumes about twenty-six pounds of carbon dioxide a year; 100 million trees can reduce the carbon dioxide in the atmosphere by 18 million tons.

New York City school children plant a tree as part of an environmental campaign. In the back row are Mayor David Dinkins (left) and Governor Mario Cuomo.

Tree-planting programs are already underway in many parts of the country. California groups, organized by the Trust for Public Land in San Francisco, are seeking pledges to plant 20 million trees during the decade of the 1990s. The state of North Dakota has pledged to plant 10 million trees a year, also during the 1990s. That's one hundred million trees, which is one million for each year of North Dakota's one hundred years of statehood.

The dangers of global warming are so severe that many countries of the world held international conferences on the subject in 1989. One such conference, in the Netherlands, drew delegates from more than seventy nations, including the leading producers of greenhouse gases. These nations agreed to keep future carbon-dioxide emissions in check. They also set ambitious goals for the planting of new forests. Such steps may help to halt the greenhouse effect.

Scientists, environmentalists, and government officials agree that there is no greater threat to our planet than global warming. But right now, the catastrophes such warming could trigger are merely scientific forecasts. Through international cooperation, they could remain just that.

5
Chernobyl Meltdown

The village of Chernobyl, in what was once the Soviet Union, stands empty today, long since evacuated after a fire and an explosion in one of its nuclear plants brought death and suffering to thousands and spewed a vapor cloud of radioactivity that drifted over much of the planet. Now, years after the disaster, scientists throughout the world continue to assess the tragic damage of history's worst nuclear accident.

"We still aren't sure what Chernobyl is responsible for," says Vladimir Maltsev, a health official in one of the rural areas most seriously affected. "But we know things are worse than we thought."

During the early morning hours of April 26, 1986, operators of Chernobyl's Reactor No. 4 began conducting an experiment. They wanted to find out how long the turbine generators could

An aerial view of the damaged reactor at the Chernobyl nuclear power plant.

provide electricity to the plant systems in the event of a loss of power. In the nuclear industry, this is known as a "turbine tripping experiment."

Because the operators were not well-trained and because the reactor was poorly designed, the cooling system of the reactor failed and its core overheated, triggering an uncontrolled chain reaction. Power surged and the core melted down. Two massive explosions ripped through the plant. At least thirty fires broke out.

A deadly plume of radioactive smoke and vapor shot into the air—ten times more radioactive material than was released at Hiroshima following the A-bomb blast there.

Within minutes, the nuclear plant's twenty-nine-man firefighting force arrived. "There were flashes

59

of light springing from place to place," one of the firefighters reported, "substances burning, luminescent, like sparklers."

The firefighters were on the scene for only a minute or two before their skin started turning brown from nuclear radiation. All twenty-nine men would die of radiation sickness within ten weeks. Today, their bodies emit radiation from their graves.

Other firefighting units were called in from as far away as the city of Kiev, some eighty miles to the south. By dawn, all of the fires had been extinguished, except one at the reactor core. That fire continued to burn for weeks.

At first, the directors of the plant refused to admit the reactor had been destroyed. They also refused to believe the plant's radiation monitoring systems: the needles were jumping off their dials. When civil defense officials pleaded for permission to evacuate the nearby town of Pripyat, where workers and their families lived, plant officials said no. "Don't start a panic," they said.

The day of the accident was bright and sunny in Pripyat. Children were permitted to go to school. Later in the day, they played soccer in the streets. Not until the day after the accident did authorities agree to move the people out of Pripyat. They waited more than a week to evacuate the rest of the area around Chernobyl.

Meanwhile, the cloud of radioactive particles, which was riding shifting winds, drifted north across the Soviet Union. Then it moved beyond,

A Soviet medical technician checks a young child for radiation during inspection of the residents of the village of Kopylovo, near Kiev.

over the Scandinavian countries of Sweden, Norway, and Denmark. Later, as weather conditions changed, the Ukraine and other parts of Europe were threatened.

Humans can be affected by radioactivity in several different ways — by simply being exposed to a passing cloud or breathing in radioactive particles, by exposure to radioactive soil, or by eating contaminated food or drinking contaminated water.

From studies of the victims at Hiroshima and Nagasaki, scientists know what to expect from radiation poisoning. Many residents of those two cities who appeared unharmed immediately after the bomb blast soon developed acute radiation sickness. They complained of nausea, dizziness,

61

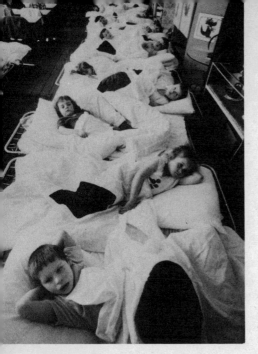

Young victims of Chernobyl in a hospital ward in Syekova, not far from the reactor site.

and headaches. They went on to suffer hemor-rhaging, intestinal problems, and loss of hair. Severe complications led to death.

But radiation damage can also be long-term, with the effects not evident for years. Cancer is one effect of radiation poisoning. A person's genes can also be damaged. This causes harmful traits to be passed to the person's children.

For almost two full days after the Chernobyl disaster, the leaders of the Soviet Union said nothing. The outside world got its first clue when a worker at a Swedish nuclear-power plant walked past a radiation detector and set off an alarm. Radiation was discovered on covers he wore over his shoes. Officials quickly evacuated the plant. Soon after, they determined there was nothing wrong with it.

Then monitoring stations elsewhere in Sweden began reporting a sudden jump in radiation levels. As more evidence came in, Swedish officials determined a cloud of radioactivity had drifted over their country. By Monday, the cloud had been traced back to the south, to Chernobyl. That evening, Soviet officials admitted that an accident had taken place but gave no details.

In the days that followed, radiation levels rose in many countries. Poland banned the sale of milk from cows that had eaten grass in the fields. Children were made to take doses of iodine to guard against cancer of the thyroid, a gland that regulates growth. Farmers as far away as Italy and Sweden were forced to destroy field-grown vegetables and fruit.

Radioactivity from Chernobyl made the town of Gavle, Sweden, and the area surrounding it, more radioactive than any other place in Europe. Radioactive readings were four times those of West Germany and ten times as high as Norway's. Radioactivity was detected in reindeer, in fish found in streams and lakes, and in both the hay that cows ate and their milk.

The winds carried radiation over Lapland, a vast European wilderness located some eleven hundred miles from Chernobyl that extends across the northern parts of Norway, Sweden, and Finland, and the extreme northwestern corner of the

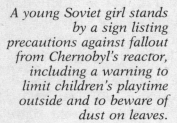

A young Soviet girl stands by a sign listing precautions against fallout from Chernobyl's reactor, including a warning to limit children's playtime outside and to beware of dust on leaves.

former Soviet Union. The Arctic Circle is just to the north.

The radioactive cloud from Chernobyl poisoned the pastures of northern reindeer, which are a cornerstone of Lapland's economy. Tiny, blue-green plants called lichens, the reindeer's basic food, absorbed radioactivity from the spring rains. When the reindeer people from Klimpfjall, Sweden, gathered their flocks late in the summer of 1986, and slaughtered some of the animals for food and for sale, they found the animals contained ten to forty times more radioactivity than permitted for human consumption.

No one could say when the animals would be healthy again. Some experts said the deer would remain contaminated well into the 1990s.

In the weeks following the accident, low levels of fallout were measured on the West Coast of the United States. In the Pacific Northwest, the states of Oregon and Washington advised against drinking rainwater, although the amount of radioactivity it contained was not believed to be high. A resident of Oregon drinking a quart of rainwater would get about the same amount of radioactivity as in two-and-one-half chest X rays. Throughout the Pacific Northwest, sales of bottled water shot up.

In Canada, health officials discovered traces of radioactivity in rainfall all the way from Vancouver on the west coast to St. John's, Newfoundland in the east. Health minister Jake Epp announced that his inspectors were monitoring milk across the country for contamination and examining vegetables for radioactivity. He warned Canadians not to drink rainwater. "There is no need for panic," said Epp. "There is a need for vigilance."

Today, Chernobyl's Reactor No. 4 is cloaked in a blackened concrete shell, a huge structure, ten stories high. For eighteen miles around, the massive tomb is surrounded by barbed wire. Only those on official business are permitted to enter. This is a "forbidden zone."

Within what was once the Soviet Union, a wide stretch of land the size of Holland has been permanently poisoned. About two hundred thousand people have been evacuated from their homes. But

Firemen in Germany wash down a truck after discovering radioactive contamination that had spread from Chernobyl.

nearly 5 million people still live in contaminated areas.

Enormous numbers of people may yet be victims of the Chernobyl meltdown. The early 1990s saw a dramatic rise in birth defects in Byelorussia, a republic the size of the state of Kansas. "A baby was born with six fingers the other day," a doctor told *The New York Times* in 1991. "Another was born without an ear." Childhood leukemia, a cancerous disease of the blood, also showed a sharp increase. Two million people in Byelorussia, including 800,000 children, still live in contaminated areas.

Dr. Robert Gale of the University of California at Los Angeles helped to treat Chernobyl victims in Moscow in the weeks following the explosion. He has estimated that between two thousand and twenty thousand Russian people will die in the next fifty years as a result of the accident.

John Gofman, professor of biophysics at the University of California at Berkeley, has predicted that Chernobyl will eventually cause between fifty thousand and two hundred fifty thousand deaths in what was once the Soviet Union. He also says that an equal number of people will die outside of that nation's borders.

Chernobyl proved once and for all: A nuclear accident anywhere is a nuclear accident *everywhere*.

It's the same with other airborne toxic chemicals. For instance, the pesticide toxaphene has been banned in the United States because of its cancer-causing properties. The chemical, used by farmers in Latin America to kill grubs that destroy corn roots, has been detected in the waters of Lake Superior and in the fish that live there.

Lee Liebenstein, a specialist in toxic substances at the state of Wisconsin's Department of Natural Resources, believes toxaphene rides the winds — the storm systems that sweep up from the Gulf of Mexico and veer over Oklahoma and into the states bordering the Great Lakes. If Liebenstein is right, toxaphene is, to quote the National Wildlife Federation, "one of the latest international terrorists."

Like human terrorists, pollutants cross political

boundaries freely. No place on earth is safe from their threat.

Another example of what's happening is the ozone layer, an invisible shield of gas up in the sky, more than twelve miles above the earth, that protects us from the sun's harmful ultraviolet radiation. Within the past decade, scientists discovered that the ozone layer has been severely damaged by chemical products we use. These chemicals, chiefly chloroflurocarbons (CFCs) are used as coolants in refrigerators and air conditioners. They are also used as solvents and as propellants in aerosol cans.

The big problem with CFCs is that, once they've escaped into the atmosphere, nothing happens to them. They don't dissolve in the rain. They aren't destroyed by sunlight. They don't react with other gases. Some of the CFCs being released today will still be in the atmosphere a century from now.

Once they've floated upward to the stratosphere, the CFCs break apart, releasing one of their components, chlorine. It's the chlorine atoms that gobble up the thin layer of ozone. In fact, a single atom of chlorine can destroy more than one hundred thousand molecules of ozone.

During the 1970s, scientists began warning that CFCs could attack the ozone. Several countries, including the United States, Canada, Norway, and Sweden, responded to the warning by banning CFCs in spray cans. Spray cans are still in widespread use, of course, but manufacturers in the

United States and some other countries have switched from CFCs to other gases. But many nations did nothing. At the same time, industries were finding new uses for CFCs. So despite the ban on CFCs in spray cans, the threat to the ozone layer did not lessen.

In 1985 came the really bad news. Scientists learned that an actual hole had been found in the ozone layer above the continent of Antarctica.

The situation keeps getting worse. In 1991, the Environmental Protection Agency announced that, in many areas of the globe, the ozone loss was taking place more than twice as fast as had been expected. And early in 1992, detectors aboard a converted spy plane flying over New England and eastern Canada recorded the highest level of ozone-thinning chlorine ever measured anywhere around the globe. The level was 50 percent higher than the amount recorded over Antarctica, the site of the huge ozone hole discovery in 1985.

We need the protection of the ozone layer. Without it, ultraviolet radiation could trigger a big increase in skin cancer and in cataracts, damage to the eye that can lead to blindness. According to one estimate, an additional half-million cases of skin cancer could result.

Toxic chemicals drifting from one nation to another, a damaging thinning of the ozone layer, and radioactive fallout are all *global* threats. As such, they require global solutions.

As the world enters the final decade of the twentieth century, humans find themselves at a critical turning point. Our survival is at stake. As Lester Brown, president of the Worldwatch Institute stated: "We do not have generations, we only have years in which to attempt to turn things around."

6
Beachless Summer

During the summer of 1988, thousands of New Yorkers seeking to escape the sweltering heat of the hazy, humid city, sought out the area's public beaches. What they found, to their horror and disgust, was a sickening array of medical waste being washed up onto the shore by the incoming tides.

The flood of stained bandages, blood-filled vials, plastic pill containers, and syringes with needles ruined the summer for thousands of beachgoers. Red flags and warning signs became familiar sights as beaches opened, closed, reopened, and then closed again.

From Montauk, at the eastern end of Long Island, to Cape May, New Jersey, beach attendance nosedived. As the trash continued to foul the beaches, officials in several states tried to track down its source. Investigators sifted through the

A park supervisor holds a syringe found on a Rockaway, New York, beach in July, 1988.

debris, looking for labels, markings, or anything else that might serve as a clue.

It didn't take long to establish that most of the waste had come from a medical facility of some kind — a hospital, clinic, or laboratory. But who dumped it?

Under New York State law, hospital wastes known to be infectious must be placed in special red bags. Some hospitals burn such wastes in their own incinerators. Others use private garbage-carting companies to truck the waste to a licensed incinerator or a special disposal site.

According to one theory, a hospital, clinic, or lab paid a private carter to haul away its trash to an approved incinerator. But the carter, to save money, simply backed the truck down a pier and dumped the trash into New York Harbor. The winds and tides did the rest.

Major hospitals were not suspected. A hospital, said one official, "would not be stupid enough to open the back door and throw the stuff in the water."

Another investigator blamed unlicensed medical facilities. He called them "fly-by-night clinics."

In the end, investigators were unable to establish a single source for the beach waste. Said one official: "It's like finding a ball at the bottom of a hill, and there are thirty houses on the hill. It could come from any one of them."

To help curb the problem of polluted beaches, officials requested stiffer penalties for illegal dumpers. They asked for more incinerators and more sewage-treatment plants. Annual beach cleanups also help. But even the most optimistic realized it would be several years before the problem would be completely solved.

America is often called a "disposable society." We like to use cheap and convenient products that we soon toss out.

The needles on medical syringes are one example. Not so long ago, they were used again and again. Of course, the needles had to be sterilized before each use. Disposable needles are much easier for the medical profession. They're already sterilized. But they create problems when it comes to getting rid of them (as many beachgoers in the Northeast can testify).

A Babylon, New York, councilman searches one of the town's beaches for medical debris during the summer of 1988.

The throwaway lifestyle is often typified by plastic products. Lighter than metals, more durable than wood, and safer than glass, plastic is America's favorite material.

For evidence of this, all you have to do is visit almost any ocean beach and notice how much plastic debris washes ashore. Some beaches are flooded with it. In a three-hour cleanup on the sands of the Texas Gulf Coast one afternoon in September 1987, volunteers collected 307 tons of litter, two-thirds of which was plastic. It included 31,733 plastic bags, 30,295 plastic bottles, 1,914 disposable diapers, and 7,460 plastic milk jugs.

Plastic debris is a hazard to small boats. Plastic rope and fishing line get caught in boat propellers. Plastic bags and sheets of plastic clog water intakes, which can lead to engine failure.

But while plastic debris is usually little more than a nuisance to boaters, it can seriously injure or even kill marine life. As many as two million seabirds and one hundred thousand seals, sea lions, and sea otters die every year after becoming entangled in plastic debris. Plastic also has a deadly effect on whales, dolphins, porpoises, and sea otters. "You can go to an oil spill or toxic chemical spill and see animals struggling to survive," David Laist, an analyst for the U.S. Marine Mammal Commission, told *Smithsonian* magazine. "But those dangers are concentrated in one place. With plastic pollution, it's a different situation. Plastics are like individual mines floating around the ocean just waiting for victims."

What often happens is that marine animals confuse plastic items for food. Seabirds are known to eat everything from plastic caps and lids to plastic cigarette lighters. Some birds even feed small plastic pieces to their young. Once swallowed, a piece of plastic can cause internal injury or block the bird's intestinal tract. In either case, starvation and death can be the result.

Sea turtles often mistake plastic bags or plastic sheeting for jellyfish, plankton, newly hatched crabs, or other forms of prey. Once in the turtle's intestines, the material not only wrecks the animal's digestive system, but it makes the turtle too buoyant to dive for food. A pitiful death follows.

Even whales are victims. They have been found dead with plastic bags and sheeting in their stomachs. When a young sperm whale beached itself on Galveston Island in the Gulf of Mexico, it was taken to an aquarium and studied. The animal seemed to be healthy, eating squid and diving playfully in its holding tank. Suddenly, the whale stopped eating and died. When marine biologists examined the animal in an effort to learn the cause of its death, it was found to have an internal infection. And no wonder. In the whale's stomach they found a garbage-can liner, a plastic bread wrapper, and a corn chip bag.

Swallowing plastic is only part of the problem. Thousands of sea birds and animals die every year from getting entangled in plastic debris. Unable to escape, the animal eventually drowns, starves to death, or dies from exhaustion in its frenzied attempt to free itself. Brown pelicans, for example, become so entangled in fishing lines that they end up hanging themselves.

Young seals are often attracted to plastic trash floating in the water. They sometimes get their necks caught in plastic netting or the plastic yokes that hold six-packs of soda or beer together. A seal can grow up wearing a plastic collar, which gets tighter and tighter as the seal's neck gets larger. In time, the plastic can strangle the animal.

Sources of plastic pollution include commercial fishermen, merchant ships, passenger liners, military vessels, pleasure boats, and offshore oil and gas drilling operations. If you are out on a boat, remember: Never discard anything overboard.

Girl Scout volunteers pitch in to help clean up a Sandy Hook, New Jersey, beach.

Urge others to keep plastics and other trash out of the ocean and waterways.

Beginning in January 1989, it became illegal for boats and ships to dispose of plastics — anything from plastic cups to garbage bags — anywhere in the oceans or other navigable waters of the United States. Violaters caught dumping can be fined up to $25,000. Illegal dumping should be reported to the local Coast Guard commander.

You don't have to be aboard a boat to help solve this problem. Anytime you visit a beach, take along a garbage bag. Fill it with any debris you might happen to find — plastic cups and eating utensils, plastic bags and bottles, plastic caps and lids, pieces of foam plastic, and plastic six-pack rings.

Once the bag is filled, throw it in a garbage can. Also pick up any other litter you find on the beach. Glass bottles and aluminum cans can be recycled.

Every year, the Center for Marine Conservation in Washington, DC, sponsors a national beach cleanup. For several hours on a September afternoon, volunteers in twenty-five coastal states and parts of Canada and Mexico pick up trash on local beaches. In recent years, millions of pounds of garbage have been collected and countless sea birds and sea animals have been saved as a result.

The Center for Marine Conservation encourages young people to take part in the cleanup program. Write for more information, and request the date for this year's cleanup in your state.

7
Tragedy in Alaska

In the 1960s, huge deposits of oil were found in Alaska. As drilling was about to begin, the oil industry faced a tough problem: How do you get all that oil from Alaska's North Slope to the oil refineries in the lower forty-eight states?

The oil industry proposed a pipeline that would link Prudhoe Bay on the North Slope to the Alaskan port of Valdez in the south. From Valdez (pronounced *val-deez*), supertankers would then haul the crude oil to ports on the West Coast of the United States where refineries were located.

Environmentalists fought this plan. They insisted that the pipeline should go from Prudhoe Bay through Canada into the lower forty-eight states. The environmentalists wanted to avoid shipping large quantities of oil from Valdez, with its icebergs, reefs, and storms. The Sierra Club, for example, predicted "major mishaps, spills, and casualties."

But the oil companies promised to apply modern technology to tanker navigation and oilspill cleanup. The fears of environmentalists were obsolete, they claimed.

When the U.S. Senate voted on the oil industry's plan for the pipeline, the result was a 49–49 tie. It was then up to Spiro Agnew, the nation's vice-president at the time and, as such, the president of the Senate, to cast the vote that would break the deadlock. On July 17, 1973, Agnew, reflecting the Nixon administration's support of the oil industry, broke the tie by voting in favor of building the pipeline to Valdez.

The pipeline began operation in 1977. Eventually, as much as 2.1 million barrels a day flowed through the pipeline to Valdez, where the tankers were loaded.

In the early years, tight rules were in effect governing tanker operations and no mishaps occurred. But little by little, regulations were relaxed or even completely disregarded. At first, tankers were prohibited from moving at night after dark. Later that rule was lifted.

Another change had to do with pilots, trained and licensed to steer ships in dangerous waters into and out of harbors. The areas through which pilots were required to guide tankers were reduced.

That was the situation in the hours approaching midnight on March 23, 1989, when the 987-foot

Captain Joseph Hazelwood, captain of the Exxon Valdez.

Exxon Valdez, loaded with 50 million gallons of North Shore crude oil, eased away from its pier and into the darkness toward the Valdez Narrows and the waters of Prince William Sound beyond.

As required, a harbor pilot guided the ship, calling out instructions to a helmsman steering the vessel. According to witnesses, Joseph Hazelwood, the tanker's captain, had retired to his cabin, leaving third mate Gregory Cousins and seaman Robert Kagan, the helmsman, on the bridge.

Hazelwood returned to the bridge when it came time to drop off the pilot, the person qualified to steer the tanker out of Valdez. Hazelwood ordered a course change to avoid icebergs coming out of Columbia Glacier and then switched the steering mechanism to automatic pilot.

At about seven minutes before midnight, Hazelwood returned to his cabin. He left instructions for Cousins and Kagan to steer the ship back to the normal course when the vessel came abreast of Busby Island, about twenty-five miles from Valdez.

When the *Valdez*'s radar showed more icebergs, Cousins requested permission from the Coast Guard to switch from the outboard channel to the inboard channel to avoid them. Permission was granted.

Cousins then ordered Kagan to turn the ship 10° starboard (right). When the radar showed the ship was not turning, Cousins called for 20° right rudder. Still nothing happened.

When Cousins looked at the radar again, he didn't like what he saw. He telephoned Hazelwood. "I think we're in serious trouble," he said. The words were hardly out of his mouth when the night air was suddenly filled with the groaning sound of steel grinding on stone. The *Exxon Valdez* had plowed into the submerged rocks of Bligh Reef, ripping four big holes in its bottom. Immediately the ship began gushing oil into Prince William Sound, one of North America's most sensitive marine environments.

For the next three hours, the tanker poured oil into the sound at the rate of nearly one thousand gallons a second. Almost 11 million gallons escaped from the vessel, making it the biggest oil spill in U.S. history.

"There is no doubt in my mind that the long-term environmental consequences of the . . . spill will far exceed those of Chernobyl or Bhopal," Jay Hair, president of the National Wildlife Federation, told *Newsweek* magazine. "It's probably fair to say that in our lifetime we will never see the Sound the way it was on March 23, 1989."

After workers emptied the cargo tanks of the *Exxon Valdez* of remaining oil and pumped the tanks full of compressed air, six tugs pulled the huge tanker through the waters of Prince William Sound to a remote bay on Naked Island. The same day, Captain Hazelwood surrendered to authorities to face criminal charges in Alaska for operating a vessel while intoxicated and for neg-

After its accident, the Exxon Valdez *unloaded crude oil into the smaller* Exxon Baton Rouge.

ligent discharge of oil. Hazelwood was eventually acquitted in Alaska of the charges of intoxication and endangerment.

In the meantime, rescue workers and environmentalists began to survey the damage that had taken place as a result of the gooey tide of oil that had seeped into Prince William Sound. Nearly one thousand miles of coastline would become covered with thick black scum. In some areas, the oil slapped onto the beaches with such fury that "it sloshed into the trees," said one observer. The oil coated thousands of marine mammals and birds, and threatened Alaska's fishing industry.

When it came to cleaning up the spill, confusion ruled the day. The cleanup was the responsibility of the Alyeska Pipeline Service Company, an association of oil companies operating the pipeline terminals.

Alyeska's plan involved a three-pronged attack. First, they would "boom it" — surround it with floating barriers meant to contain the oil and hold it in check. Second, they intended to skim the oil off. Using vacuum-cleaner type machines mounted on boats, they would suck up any oil that floated on the surface. The third method of attack was for the oil they couldn't boom or skim. This they planned to burn or scatter with dispersants, detergent-like chemicals that break down the oil slick into little droplets that eventually sink.

It sounded good on paper. Reality was much different. For example, Alyeska's plan called for any spill to be encircled with booms within three hours. But at the time of the accident, the only barge in Valdez equipped to boom the spill was in drydock to repair a big dent in its hull. The barge and the booms did not arrive at the site until ten hours after the accident.

Under the terms of the cleanup plan, Alyeska was to have seven skimmers on the scene within five hours. Instead, it took twelve hours to get just three skimmers there, and those three did not begin work for another eighteen hours.

There were also long delays in applying the dispersants. Exxon intended to spray the chemicals from planes and helicopters, but the company needed approval from the Coast Guard to begin spraying. It took three days to get permission.

But getting permission was beside the point. The day of the accident, Exxon had less than four thousand gallons of chemicals on hand to use as dispersants. That wasn't nearly enough. Some five hundred thousand gallons were needed to fight a spill that size.

The fact that Alyeska wasn't ready to clean up the spill was not a great surprise to many Alaskans. *The Wall Street Journal* reported that a spill drill conducted by the state in 1984 was so fouled up that it was almost laughable. Oil booms sunk, machinery proved defective, and there was a near collision between a barge and a tanker. After an hour of turmoil, the drill was called off.

With cleanup operations lagging, it soon became clear that the spill was turning into an environmental disaster. The fishing industry was

Animal recovery crews pick up dead sea otters recovered from Green Island in Prince William Sound.

temporarily wiped out. The pictures on TV every night of dying birds and oil-soaked otters stunned the nation. President Bush called the spill "a major tragedy."

Rescue workers put in fifteen-hour days in an effort to save birds and animals caught in the oil. Volunteers helped capture and clean oil-coated cormorants, gulls, grebes, murres, and several species of ducks. The fouled birds were wrapped in towels or blankets, placed in boxes, and scrubbed with dishwashing liquid. Oil-covered birds were spotted as far away as 125 miles from the spill site, near Anchorage.

The area's five thousand sea otters were a special worry. Weighing up to ninety pounds, with sharp teeth and claws, the otters were practically defenseless when exposed to the oil, which reduced the insulation of their fur. If they did not die from the cold, they took in fatal doses of oil while trying to lick it off of their coats. At least a thousand sea otters are known to have died, and perhaps as many as three thousand.

Whales, seals, and sea lions, insulated with fat rather than feathers or fur, were better off than the otters and birds. Although none were found dead in the weeks following the spill, many sea animals killed by the oil simply sank out of sight. Many others were thought to be consuming great quantities of oil-contaminated food. No one could say what the long-term effects might be.

That summer some eleven thousand workers hired by Exxon took part in a diligent cleanup

Clean-up workers prepare to vacuum crude oil from the shore of Block Island on Prince William Sound.

campaign. They sought to clean the beaches with everything from paper towels to rakes and shovels. They also scoured the beaches with hot water, washing oil-covered rocks with powerful jets of scalding seawater. Sometimes they would make half-a-dozen passes over a single beach. The idea was to soften the oil so it would flow into the water. There it could be collected within floating booms and picked up by skimmers.

But this strategy proved as destructive as the spilled oil. Scientists later said, the hot water actually "sterilized" parts of the beaches, destroying plants, shellfish, and other marine organisms.

"At the time, it made sense," said Dr. Sylvia Earle, the chief scientist of the National Oceanic and Atmospheric Administration. "You had a great desire to do something. People were running around with towels wiping rocks."

The spill took an enormous toll on wildlife in Prince William Sound. Some colonies of murres, black and white diving birds common to the North Pacific, were all but wiped out. It is believed that about one hundred fifty thousand murres perished as a direct result of the spill. The long-term effects were every bit as destructive. According to federal scientists, murres in the spill area apparently failed to bear young in the two years following the accident. "We've seen two years of total failure," one scientist told the *Washington Post*. "It's wrong to say we lost all the murres in Alaska but . . . certain areas are greatly impacted."

In April 1992, slightly more than three years

This red-necked greb is one of many that became covered with oil after the Exxon Valdez *accident.*

after the spill, a report issued by the state and federal agencies said that fish, marine mammals, and other resources were harmed much more extensively than originally believed. Among the report's findings:

• Between thirty-five hundred and five thousand sea otters died of acute petroleum poisoning.

• Thousands of bald eagles, sea ducks, loons, cormorants, and other species have died.

• Thirty-five archaeological sites, including burial and home sites, were damaged.

The report, along with other studies published in the early 1990s, helped to make it clear that the millions of gallons of oil that gushed from the *Exxon Valdez* triggered the worst domestic environmental disaster of the 1980s.

To environmentalists what happened at Prince William Sound in 1989 is clear evidence that the oil industry has no business probing for petroleum amidst the delicate ecology of Alaska. Nevertheless, the industry is eager to expand its operations there by exploring for oil within the Arctic National Wildlife Refuge.

Located in northeastern Alaska and covering some 19 million acres, the Arctic National Wildlife Refuge is the home of a unique array of wildlife. Herds of caribou have used the coastal region as a calving area for hundreds of years. The annual gathering of the herd, which numbers in the tens of thousands, is one of nature's most exciting spectacles, reminiscent of the enormous herds of buffalo that once thundered across the Great Plains of the United States and Canada.

Grizzly bears, moose, and wolves are among the more than two hundred other animal species that live there. Millions of birds from points as distant as Chesapeake Bay and Africa nest and breed on the coastal plain.

The oil industry promises to develop the Arctic Refuge in an "environmentally sensitive" manner. But the Wilderness Society and other environmental organizations question whether such development is necessary. They point out that nearly 90 percent of Alaska's Arctic Ocean coastline is already open to oil and gas development.

To environmentalists, development means the

Sea lions frolic in the oil-coated waters of Prince William Sound some 50 miles from the tanker accident.

construction of hundreds of miles of roads and pipelines, which would disrupt the free movement of wildlife. It means toxic wastes leaking onto the fragile tundra and contaminating wetlands. It also means the arrival of thousands of workers and the creation of air pollution that will come to equal that of a small city.

President Bush supported the idea of drilling for oil in the Arctic National Wildlife Refuge. He said he saw "no connection" between the shipwreck and the question of drilling in the refuge. "We are becoming increasingly dependent on foreign oil," Mr. Bush said, "and that is not acceptable to any president."

Environmentalists point out that tapping the refuge would be no more than a "quick fix." The oil there might satisfy some of our needs for a decade or so, but then the nation would again be faced with the question of what to do next.

A better plan would be to improve the fuel efficiency of motor vehicles. That could save an amount of oil equal to, or in excess of, what may exist in the arctic refuge.

According to Amory Levins, director of research at the Rocky Mountain Institute, "Improving America's 19-mile-per-gallon household vehicle fleet by three miles per gallon could replace U.S. imports of oil from Iraq and Kuwait. Another nine miles per gallon would end the need for any oil from the Persian Gulf."

In March 1989, just days before the *Exxon Valdez* disaster, the Energy and Natural Resources Committee of the U.S. Senate voted to permit exploratory drilling in the Arctic National Wildlife Refuge. But the daily televised images of oil-soaked birds and blackened beaches derailed the legislation — for the time being. No one doubted, however, that one day the oil industry would renew its efforts to open Alaska's coastal plain to exploration and drilling.

You can play a role in this struggle. You can write to the nation's legislative leaders and let them know your feelings on this issue.

Letters play an important role. A study by Orval Hansen, president of the Columbia Institute, disclosed that the best way for individuals to influence their senators and representatives is to write letters. And according to the National Wildlife Federation, the biggest conservation group in the United States, letter writing helped to get the 1988 Endangered Species Act and Clean Water Act passed into law.

For the names of senators and representatives, consult *The World Almanac* or any current almanac, or contact your local library. Write to senators at:

> U.S. Senate
> Washington, DC
> 20510

Write to members of the House at:

> U.S. House of Representatives
> Washington, DC
> 20515

Letters to senators and house members are treated very seriously. Not only will your letter be answered, but, if it concerns a particular issue, you're likely to get a follow-up response should the congress person take action on the issue.

Letters are tabulated, too. Staff members keep track of how many letters are received in favor of a particular issue, and how many are written in opposition to it.

Every letter counts. Senator Albert Gore, Jr., the first member of Congress to fight for legislation to help reduce global warming, acknowledged the importance of letter writing when he said: "When politicians see enough people demanding action on the environment, then the laws will change."

8
Wandering Garbage

Through much of the spring and summer of 1987, a seagoing barge from Long Island, New York, reigned as the symbol of America's garbage crisis. For 155 days and more than six thousand miles at sea, the barge was unable to find a disposal site for its cargo. Six states and three foreign countries rejected the vessel's attempts to unload. "The Garbage Without a Country," it was called.

The garbage that nobody wanted was not a catastrophe in the strict sense. It did not trigger widespread disaster or distress. No one was killed or maimed.

What it did do was put the spotlight on America's garbage mess. Unsightly landfills are overflowing with rotting garbage. Toxic dumps leak hazardous chemicals into our water supplies. Incinerated wastes poison the air we breathe. The garbage barge helped to make people aware of these problems. If they are not solved, human health could be threatened and real damage to the environment could result. The garbage barge may have represented catastrophes that are to come.

The story of the wandering barge and its smelly cargo began in November 1986, when the town of Islip on Long Island was told by state officials that it could not allow its landfill to get any bigger.

Since only a limited amount of space remained for dumping, town officials announced the landfill would accept only residential trash. Commercial refuse would have to go someplace else. That meant it would have to be trucked to other land-fills, some of them in other states.

That's when Lowell Harrelson, the head of a construction company in Bay Minette, Alabama, got into the act. He believed there was gold in the enormous amounts of garbage being produced in the string of cities along the Northeast coast. Well, not gold exactly, but methane. He planned to have the garbage tightly baled, then taken by barge to North Carolina where he would allow it to age for a short time. Methane gas builds up within garbage when organic matter decays without oxygen. The gas, which is used to generate electricity, could be sold at a nice profit. Mr. Harrelson planned to start his venture with the trash available in Islip.

Late in March 1987, Mr. Harrelson leased a barge named *Mobro* from a Louisiana company and had it loaded with Islip's trash. The barge was

The tugboat Break of Dawn *and the barge* Mobro,
*loaded with more than 3,000 tons of garbage from
Islip, New York.*

then hooked to the tugboat *Break of Dawn*, which
began pulling it southward.

Unfortunately for Mr. Harrelson, citizens in
North Carolina began to suspect that the trash
might contain hazardous wastes. The day after the
barge docked in Morehead City, North Carolina,
several protestors showed up at the pier. They
brought state environmental officials with them.
They announced the barge was not welcome in
North Carolina, that it would have to leave.

As soon as word reached other states that the
barge was headed its way, state officials began receiving telephone calls from concerned citizens.
Mississippi, Alabama, Texas, Louisiana, and Florida joined the resistance movement. Said Florida
Governor Bob Martinez: "If I have the power to

prevent garbage from New York being unloaded in this state, I intend to use it."

When the barge appeared to be heading for Mexico, Mexican officials ordered the navy to keep the vessel from its ports. The barge next seemed destined to dock in Belize, a tiny Central American country. But when the world learned that Mr. Harrelson was talking to officials in Belize, the nation's prime minister took quick action. He announced the barge would not be permitted to enter the territorial waters of Belize. Planes and ships from the Belize Defense Force were ordered to look out for the barge. The Bahamas were the third nation to reject the *Mobro*.

By this time, the barge had been at sea for more than forty days and traveled over five thousand miles. When the tugboat anchored just south of Key West, Florida, a reporter from *The New York Times* went aboard to visit Captain Duffy St. Pierre and his three-man crew. "It sort of was a joke for us in the beginning," said the captain. "But now it's starting to get on the nerves."

He said he didn't care where the garbage barge ended up, just as long as it was soon. The crew members agreed.

State officials in New York City eventually softened their stand toward the barge, announcing the garbage it contained could be unloaded at the Islip landfill. Once the barge had returned, the plan was for it to dock at Long Island City. The barge's cargo would then be trucked across the borough of Queens to Islip.

This plan didn't seem to please anyone, however. Claire Schulman, the borough president of Queens, got a court order that barred the barge from docking in her borough and the trash from traveling through it. She said the garbage had been in the Caribbean and could be a health hazard.

New York's Mayor Edward Koch did more. When the barge entered New York Harbor, the mayor ordered police department launches with armed officers aboard to turn the barge away. Many people couldn't understand the mayor's reaction. After all, it was pointed out, between sixteen and eighteen bargeloads of garbage were dumped in the city's landfills every day. One more could hardly matter.

The *Mobro* and the *Break of Dawn* anchored off Brooklyn. That caused more headlines. Harold Golden, the Brooklyn borough president, threatened to ask the sanitation department to get the barge out of the waters of his borough. Said Captain St. Pierre: "All the politicians are trying to get themselves reelected on this barge."

It wasn't long before the barge became a tourist attraction. Residents of Brooklyn lined the shore, training their binoculars and telescopes on the barge and its tug. Small boats and yachts, some from neighboring states, circled the two vessels.

By this time, the barge had captured the interest of Johnny Carson, who mentioned it almost every night on his TV show. *Donahue* became interested in it, too. Phil Donahue made a field trip to the *Mobro* and was shown plodding through the bales

The bales of garbage were finally unloaded, inspected, and hauled off to an incinerator.

of trash. He called the collection, "the most famous three thousand tons of garbage in the universe." Hundreds of newspaper stories were written about the barge and its long voyage.

A judge in New York overturned the city's objections to the barge. Not long after, it was finally permitted to dock and be unloaded. "I appreciate that this brought to people's attention that there is a waste disposal problem in America," said Brendan Sexton, New York City's sanitation commissioner. "But enough is enough, it's time to end it."

Call it garbage, refuse, trash, rubbish, or junk. It's what we produce in our homes and offices that we stuff into big gray-green bags or cram into metal or plastic cans and put out for pickup.

Whatever you call it, the United States is number one in its production, and no other country is even close. It's estimated that we produce four hundred thousand tons of trash a day.

By the year 2000, according to *U.S. News & World Report*, each American will generate six pounds of refuse a day, which is about double the 1960 amount. And about one half of our trash is from packaging alone.

The United States has three ways to deal with the trash it produces: dump, burn, or recycle it. Most gets dumped. About 80 percent of the nation's solid waste goes into landfills. Ten percent gets burned; ten percent gets recycled.

Ordinary landfills are little more than open dumps that attract rats and seagulls. Rain and groundwater filter through the refuse to create an evil-smelling poisonous soup. This toxic liquid can seep into local groundwater supplies, contaminating drinking water and poisoning farmlands that draw upon it for irrigation purposes.

Somewhat better are the so-called "sanitary" landfills. Before any dumping begins, the site is lined with clay and thick sheets of plastic. "You build what amounts to a huge bathtub," says a waste-management expert.

Pipes installed under the garbage collect the toxic liquid, and a pumping system moves it to a treatment plant, where the poisonous chemicals are filtered out. Bulldozers keep busy night and day covering the trash with earth.

The biggest problem with landfills, sanitary or

otherwise, is that they are being closed because they are filling up. Nearly half of the country's six thousand landfills are scheduled to shut down during the 1990s. Already some northeastern states that have run out of landfill space are trucking their excess trash to other states — at a very high cost. Some of New York's trash, for instance, is hauled to landfills in Pennsylvania, Ohio, and Kentucky.

While new landfills are much less likely to leak toxic chemicals, and waste management experts have learned to control the bad dump odors, nobody wants one for a neighbor. "Everybody wants us to pick it up," says an official with the Environmental Protection Agency, "but nobody wants us to put it down."

Most of New York City's residential refuse goes to the Fresh Kills Landfill on Staten Island, the world's largest.

Burning garbage is an alternative, but that creates another set of problems. Most incinerators spew dust and gases into the atmosphere, although devices called "scrubbers" can reduce the amount of emissions.

But what's to be done with the residue that remains in the incinerator after burning? It often contains high levels of toxic chemicals such as lead and cadmium. A dumpsite is needed for them.

When it comes to solid wastes, used newspapers are the number-one problem, according to Congressman Richard T. Schulze of Pennsylvania. Newspapers account for about 8 percent of all landfill waste. No other single product puts so great a strain on the nation's landfills.

It's not just a landfill problem, however. Newsprint is made from wood pulp, causing precious trees to be cut down. The numbers are enormous. For example, an average printing of the Sunday edition of *The New York Times* requires seventy-five thousand trees. Congressman Schulze calls this "the needless loss of millions of acres of forest lands."

There's a partial solution to both of these problems: recycling. Today's newspaper can be processed into another newspaper or other paper products. Some newspapers are already using recycled paper.

The price of unused or virgin paper and recycled paper works out to be almost the same. But newspapers have not used great amounts of recycled paper for several reasons:

Before the barge was unloaded, members of Greenpeace, an environmental organization, draped it with this banner.

- It's a little bit darker than unused paper.
- It sometimes absorbs more ink, meaning the print or photographs "bleed" through one side of the paper to the flip side.
- Supplies of recycled paper have been limited. But now they're on the increase.

The EPA has reported that 13.3 million tons of newsprint are produced in the United States each year. Only about one third is recycled.

Some states have acted to boost that amount. Two states — Connecticut and California — have laws requiring the use of recycled newsprint. Florida taxes newspapers that use virgin newsprint.

Representative Schulze has introduced legislation in Congress that could impose stiff penalties on newspapers that do not print at least 50 percent of their circulation on recycled paper by the year 2000. The bill would also provide a 10-percent tax credit to newspapers that buy recycling equipment and machinery.

You can help. In school, get your class to write to the publisher of a local or national newspaper. Find out the amount of recycled newsprint now being used by the paper. Urge the publisher to use as much recycled newsprint as possible.

Also check the textbooks you use in school. If they're not printed on recycled paper, write to the publisher and recommend a changeover.

Plastics are another major landfill problem. It's because they're practically indestructible. The bacteria and fungi that naturally break down organic materials, such as cloth or paper, can't penetrate plastics. Plastic bottles dumped into landfills today are likely to still be there hundreds of years from now. Plastic waste also pollutes the oceans and injures wildlife.

Some manufacturers who package their products in certain types of plastic containers have sought to win the public's favor by calling them "biodegradable," meaning they will decompose by natural biological processes. But such claims have been challenged by environmental organizations.

The Center for Biology of Natural Systems at the Queens College branch of the City University of New York conducted a study for Greenpeace that took a close look at plastics containing certain additives meant to make plastic break down more easily. It found that the plastic did break into smaller pieces, but not ones small enough to be biodegradable. The volume of plastic was not reduced.

Greenpeace and other environmental groups say that terms such as biodegradable are meant to mislead consumers. Several states have supported the environmentalists by bringing legal action against some companies that make disposable diapers and plastic garbage bags and that have made hollow claims for them.

Glass and aluminum are more successfully recycled than paper or plastic. All the glass that you return for recycling is reused to make new glass. As for aluminum, Americans now recycle about two thirds of all aluminum beverage cans, approximately 55 billion cans a year. The recycled aluminum is used chiefly to make new cans.

Recycling is not a cure-all for the solid waste problem. At best, by the year 2000 recycling will be eliminating from 20 to 25 percent of the nation's trash.

Better than recycling is *precycling*. In 1989, the city government of Berkeley, California, launched a campaign to encourage consumers to buy food and other products packaged in containers made of biodegradable or recyclable materials. This means, for example, buying eggs in cardboard cartons rather than styrofoam cartons, and buying cereals, cookies, crackers, and other dry foods in boxes made of recycled cardboard. This is called "precycling." You're precycling when you buy apples and oranges, onions, or potatoes loose, not in plastic bags.

Precyclers buy beverages in glass or aluminum containers, which are easy to recycle. They avoid plastic containers that are not biodegradable, such as "squeezable" bottles that are made from different types of plastic in several layers.

Precycling involves always making the correct buying decision, whenever possible. In so doing, you prevent materials that are environmentally harmful from ever getting into the waste stream.

As another way of coping with the flood of refuse in which they are engulfed, some communities are turning to high-tech incinerators. These incinerators not only dispose of trash by burning it; they also convert the waste into energy. As of 1990, there were fourteen of these incinerators in use or under construction in various parts of the country.

Bridgeport, Connecticut, operates one such plant. It incinerates paper, plastics, and other trash at temperatures over 2,500°. Most older incinerators produce heat of around 1,500°. The high heat, plus a smokestack filtering system, help protect air quality.

Bridgeport's incinerator processes 2,250 tons of trash daily from 14 townships in Connecticut. From it, the plant produces enough electricity to satisfy 10 percent of Bridgeport's demand.

The city of Baltimore also operates a trash-to-energy incinerator. A huge structure, it's been nicknamed "the cathedral of garbage plants."

Similar plants are operating in Pinellas and Broward counties, Florida; Gloucester County, New Jersey; Claremont and Concord, New Hampshire; Millbury, North Andover, and Saugus, Massachusetts; Spokane, Washington; and Peekskill, New York.

Obviously, there is no single remedy to the trash problem. Smarter shopping, recycling, burning trash for energy, and continued use of what landfills remain are all important.

Citizens everywhere need to be involved in finding out what works for their community. Unless that happens, the Long Island garbage barge that cruised for six thousand miles during the summer of 1987 may come to rank as the first of a growing fleet of garbage carriers without a home.

9
The Poison Cloud

Sunday, December 2, 1984, seemed like any other day at the Union Carbide plant on the northern edge of Bhopal, a fast-growing city of over nine hundred thousand in central India. The plant produced pesticides from various chemicals, one of which was methyl isocyanate (MIC), a deadly poison.

The MIC production unit was shut down that fateful Sunday and night workers were performing routine tasks, such as washing out the pipes connected to the plant's three huge stainless steel storage tanks — most of which were underground to prevent leakage. Suddenly, some of the workers smelled bitter fumes and realized that MIC was leaking into the air. But no one could spot the source of the leak.

The workers were not alarmed. They thought it

was a "normal" leak, the kind that often occurred at the plant. When the night superintendent was told of the trouble, he shrugged. It was time for a tea break, he said. He would look for the leak afterward.

The acid smell of MIC kept getting stronger. Workers noted that temperature and pressure gauges for storage tank 610 had shot to maximum levels.

At around half past midnight, a worker ran to investigate. But it was already too late. Water had somehow gotten to the tank and a massive chemical reaction was taking place, creating tremendous heat and pressure. The ground rumbled and shook. The concrete above the tank cracked. An earsplitting hissing sound filled the air, a signal that deadly gas was escaping.

Workers now realized that they had a crisis on their hands. They turned to the plant's safety system — but in vain. A flare tower, which could be used to burn off the escaping gas, was not connected to the tank. They considered dumping the contaminated MIC into a tank that was supposed to be available as a spare, but it was already partly full. Using the tank would worsen the problem. Their last hope was to douse the leak with water. But when they turned on the spray, the water reached only one hundred feet into the air, and the gas was spewing into the air from a stack at least twenty feet higher. The workers panicked and fled.

A thick fog of death began to spread over much

of Bhopal. In the slums and shanty towns that surrounded the plant on three sides, hundreds died as they slept. Others were awakened by terrible pains in the chest. "It was like breathing fire," said one victim.

The night air was cool; there was almost no wind. Not far from the plant, a farmer was lying on his bed when he heard several thumps and realized that his cows were milling about. He got up and went outside. Two cows were lying dead on the ground. A third collapsed as he watched. Then the farmer's eyes began to burn. He ran into the darkness. The next day at a hospital, with his eyes shut and tears streaming down his face, he described how bewildered he had been. "I thought it was a plague," he said.

Thousands of people ran through the city streets, seeking escape. Some thought Bhopal had been struck by a nuclear bomb; others believed it was an earthquake. The people coughed, screamed, and called out to one another. It turned into a human stampede. People fell down, slammed into one another, and stumbled over bodies in the street as they tried to flee.

But there was no escaping the great cloud of poison. It burned the eyes, blinding thousands. It seared the lungs. The more one gasped for air, the harder it became to breathe. People vomited uncontrollably, shook violently, and fell dead.

"People were running every which way," one man recalled. "Before I knew what had happened, my wife and my brother-in-law were gone. I went back to look for them, but I fell down and I couldn't breathe. After ten minutes, I gathered all my will and forced myself to stand up again. Then I began running. I got a ride in a car to Ambarkar Nagar, about ten kilometers [6.2 miles] away from here. There I collapsed and was unconscious for an hour."

At around 2 A.M., the siren at the pesticide plant went off. Thinking that a fire had broken out, hundreds rushed toward the factory. They ran straight into the blinding gas.

Hamidia Hospital, in the center of Bhopal, was soon overflowing with weeping, moaning victims, some of them still vomiting. They filled every corner of the hospital. They lay on the floors of rooms and in hallways and were even placed out-

A mother and child await treatment outside a hospital in Bhopal.

side on the lawns. "Most people had lost a daughter or son," one doctor recalled, "or maybe a mother or a father. None of the families was complete."

Many of the doctors had been exposed to the gas and were unable to help. Medical students and policemen had to be brought in from nearby towns.

About the only way doctors could deal with victims was to wash out their eyes. Those who inhaled the gas were permitted to breathe air-rich oxygen. But the hospital had only a small number of oxygen cylinders, and thousands of patients.

The next morning, buildings remained undamaged, but the bodies of humans and animals littered the ground. They lay in roadways and alleys. Outside of the city's mortuaries, they were stacked in piles. Bhopal was a city of corpses. Vultures circled overhead for days.

The number of people who died may never be known. Most newspaper and magazine accounts of the disaster put the figure at around four thousand. In Bhopal itself, according to Larry Everest's *Behind the Poison Cloud*, "popular estimates range from 5,000 to 10,000."

Tens of thousands of survivors are still afflicted with a variety of ailments. Their lungs were burned, their eyes were charred, and their nervous systems were damaged. Years after the tragedy, *The Times of India* declared: "For many Indians, the accident has come to mean medical cases halfway between life and death . . ." A year after the

Kasturai Bai, who lost her husband, two sons, and four grandchildren in the Bhopal accident, holds a poster of some of the victims. Bai now lives in a one-room mud house across the street from the plant.

accident, some 60,000 victims were still receiving treatment at Bhopal's hospitals.

The gas leak at Bhopal that left thousands dead and perhaps as many as two hundred thousand injured ranks as one of the worst industrial accidents in history. What caused it? Who was to blame?

In the months that followed, investigators from both India and the United States sought to answer those questions. Here are some of their findings:

• Some important safety systems had never been installed at Bhopal. At a Union Carbide plant in Bezier, France, for instance, the area where MIC is stored is automatically monitored for leaks. Sensors are capable of measuring contamination in terms of hundredths of a part per million. Should a leak occur, the censors trigger alarms and automatic safety systems. Union Carbide's plant in Institute, West Virginia, where MIC is produced, is equipped with a "toxic alarm system which identifies precise locations of release."

At Bhopal, it was different. "The plant relies heavily on manual control and checking of levels," said a Union Carbide study performed two years before the disaster. Or, as Larry Everest said in *Behind the Poison Cloud*, "In Bhopal, the workers were the leak detectors."

• Leaky valves had been a constant problem at the Bhopal plant, where six serious accidents had occurred between 1978 and 1982. Three of them involved gas leaks.

• Some important safety systems were not working at the time the accident took place. Refrigeration units that were supposed to keep the MIC cool so it would not vaporize had broken down some five months before the accident and had never been repaired.

• Other safety systems were not designed to handle an emergency the size of the one that took place in the early morning hours of December 3. A flare tower, meant to burn off escaping gases, was designed to handle only small quantities of gas. According to the plant's safety manager, if workers had tried to light the flare tower while enormous quantities of flammable gases were rushing in, the result would have been a massive explosion.

115

Water sprays designed to douse the escaping gas and render it harmless also failed. Workers turned the spray on the night of the accident, but it could not reach the escaping gas. A safety-inspection report prepared by Union Carbide in 1982 recommended that more powerful sprays be installed. They never were.

• The heart of the safety system was a "vent-gas scrubber," a device that was designed to chemically cleanse escaping gas. It, too, was inadequate, only able to handle "normal" leaks.

The scrubber at Bhopal had a "feed rate" of one hundred ninety pounds per hour. On the morning of December 3, gas poured into the scrubber at the rate of more than forty thousand pounds per hour. That's two hundred times the rate for which the system was designed. A vent-gas scrubber at the Union Carbide plant in Institute, West Virginia, has a capacity of sixty thousand pounds per hour.

Not long after the accident, *Newsweek* magazine cited the differences between the Bhopal plant and other chemical plants in the United States and Europe. In these plants, a computerized early warning system "senses leaks when they occur, monitors their rate, concentration, and toxicity, evaluates weather conditions, and displays the anticipated cloud on a computer screen with the degree of danger for anything in its path." At Bhopal the plant's only computer was used in preparing the employee payroll and billing company customers. The only controls were hand controls. On the morning of December 3, workers seeking to operate the controls could only do so while enveloped in the cloud of poison gas.

After Union Carbide had completed its investigation of the accident, its Chairman, Warren Anderson, held a press conference at the company's headquarters in Danbury, Connecticut, to announce what had gone wrong. He said the accident had been caused by violations of plant safety procedures. "That plant should not have been operating," he declared.

The company had provided the necessary safeguards, Mr. Anderson added. If the Indians failed to put them into effect, they are the ones who must be held accountable: "Safety is the responsibility of the people who operate our plants," he said. "You can't be there day in and day out."

Indian officials were quick to dispute what Mr. Warren had said. "We expected he would try to palm off the blame," Kamal Pareek, an Indian engineer familiar with the Bhopal plant, told *The New York Times*. "But they cannot escape responsibility."

Others agreed that Union Carbide should be made to accept most of the blame. Larry Everest (*Behind the Poison Cloud*) declared that the "major reason" for the massacre at Bhopal was: "way too little technology in the plant's basic design." And that, he said, was Union Carbide's fault.

* * *

In 1989, a crowd of 3,000 who had suffered in the accident demonstrated in Bhopal.

Could it happen here? Could a disaster similar to the one that took place in Bhopal occur in the United States?

The chemical-industry experts say that it's not likely. Plants in the United States manufacturing pesticides and other toxic substances have emergency warning systems much more sophisticated than the one in Bhopal.

But the experts also say that the potential for danger is enormous. According to the Congressional Research Service, about 75 percent of the United States population lives "in proximity" to a chemical plant. Many of these plants manufacture hazardous pesticides. The United States is, in fact, the world's biggest producer — and user — of pesticides.

118

Pesticides are chemicals used to kill pests — flies and mosquitos, mice and rats. Farmers use them to keep pests from destroying their crops. If you've ever given your pet dog a shampoo to kill fleas, you've probably used a pesticide.

Thanks to pesticides, insect-related diseases such as malaria have been nearly wiped out. Crops have been saved from destruction.

But pesticides are made from chemicals that are poisonous. They present a wide range of hazards. Traces of pesticides can be found on the fresh fruits or vegetables you eat. When it rains, pesticides wash off the plants and into the ground and groundwater. Particles of sprayed pesticides float in the air.

No matter where they end up, pesticides are hazardous. People who drink water tainted with pesticides or who inhale contaminated air run the highest risk. It is believed that some pesticides can cause cancer and or birth defects.

Despite the hazards, there is an enormous demand for pesticides. In fact, acording to the Environmental Protection Agency, people are using ten-times more pesticides today than they did forty years ago.

And accidents do occur at these plants. They are not the size of the Bhopal disaster, to be sure. But they do cause pain and suffering.

For example, in November 1984, a small amount of MIC spilled at a pesticide plant operated by the FMC Corporation in Middleport, New York. Vapors got into the ventilation system of a school about half a mile from the spill site. Five hundred children and their teachers were evacuated. But nine children and two teachers went to the hospital with eye irritation and breathing problems. Afterward, the Middleport's fire chief complained about the "lapse of time" between the spill and the alerting of school officials, ambulance teams, and the police and fire departments.

Two months after the accident at Middleport, the disaster at Bhopal took place. Only then did Middleport residents come to realize that a very lethal chemical — MIC — was being stored and handled right in their own community.

The U.S. Occupational Safety and Health Administration (OSHA) conducted an investigation of the Middleport plant. It found the FMC Corporation to be guilty of four serious violations. According to OSHA, the plant did not have the necessary safety systems to prevent an uncontrolled chemical reaction of MIC similar to the one that triggered the Bhopal tragedy. OSHA added, however, that the chance of such an accident taking place was "extremely remote."

OSHA also revealed that four recorded leakages of MIC had taken place in Middleport since 1982. FMC installed new safety systems at the plant. But even with these in place, the plant continued to release small amounts of MIC year-round, simply as a result of normal operations, according to New York's Department of Environmental Conservation.

Union Carbide's MIC production plant in Institute, West Virginia, has been another source of dangerous chemical leakage. After the accident in Bhopal, Union Carbide shut down the plant and installed a modern computerized detection-system at the Institute plant. But on August 11, 1985, the system failed. A cloud of hazadous chemicals, at least one of which contained small amounts of MIC, escaped from a storage tank and spread over four communities. More than one hundred people had to be treated at local hospitals for burning eyes, noses, throats, and lungs.

What went wrong? Why weren't area residents told of the leak? It was because the plant officials had not programmed the computer to detect the particular gases that had escaped. By the time they realized their error, hundreds of people had been exposed to the toxic cloud.

A far greater number of people were involved when a chemical fire engulfed a California pesticide warehouse on June 22, 1985. The fire led to the evacuation of about ten thousand people in Fullerton, Placentia, and Anaheim. Those who inhaled the fumes complained of eye irritation, breathing problems, sore throats, and dizziness.

And just a few days later, a warehouse in Coachilla, California, where pesticides were stored, caught fire and exploded. Two thousand people in an area covering nine square miles had to be evacuated.

Despite improved safety systems and well-trained workers, accidents continue to occur. Speaking of Union Carbide's chemical plant in Institute, West Virginia, Jackson Browning, the company's vice president for Health, Safety, and Environmental Affairs, told a congressional committee in 1985, "Nobody wants a leak to occur. But to operate the plant without any leak for any length of time is just beyond our capabilities."

The situation is not quite as hopeless as that statement might suggest. Citizens seeking to monitor and control plants producing toxic chemicals were recently given a new weapon. It's the Emergency Planning and Community Right to Know Act. It requires manufacturers to report the total amount of each of some 330 toxic chemicals that have been released by the company into the air, water, or land.

The Community Right to Know Act came about as a result of the disaster at Bhopal. It was passed by Congress despite stiff opposition from companies that manufacture chemicals.

One of the law's most powerful results has been to make companies aware of the amount of their toxic wastes and the effect their emissions may be having on the health of local citizens.

In 1989, the Environmental Protection Agency (EPA) released the first inventory prepared according to the terms of the new law. It showed that billions of pounds of toxic chemicals had been released since 1987. As a result, some of the nation's largest companies began voluntary programs to reduce pollution.

A second inventory was made public in 1990. Afterward, the EPA asked six hundred companies to cut in half their emissions of seventeen of the

122

most dangerous toxic chemicals by 1995. "If we succeed," said William K. Reilly, the administrator of the EPA, "this program could set the pace for a new cooperative way of addressing the nation's environmental goals."

The chemical industry has perhaps the best safety record of any industry in the United States. But the risk for disaster is always there.

Right-to-know and freedom-of-information laws cannot solve the problems presented by plants manufacturing pesticides. But they help to make people more informed. Once armed with information, citizens are equipped to judge whether such plants should be allowed to operate in their communities. And in the case of existing plants, informed citizens are better able to regulate and control their operation. For example, some experts say that safety zones should be established around plants involved in the manufacture of hazardous chemicals.

What happened at Bhopal in 1984 serves as a spur for stronger regulations covering the manufacture of hazardous chemicals in the United States and other parts of the world. The process is long and slow. But only by taking action can future disasters be prevented.

10
Environmental Terrorism

Operation Desert Storm, President George Bush's name for the 1991 war to drive Iraqi forces out of Kuwait, produced a stunning victory for the United States and its allies. Within just six weeks, from mid-January to early March, the army of Saddam Hussein, the Iraqi leader, was defeated.

Americans were filled with relief and joy when the ceasefire was announced. In the weeks that followed, the first of the five hundred forty thousand U.S. military men and women arrived home from the gulf. There were patriotic celebrations all across the country. Bands played and people cheered.

But, to many of the world's scientists and environmentalists, the war in the Persian Gulf was anything but a success. It poisoned the air, land, and sea, and could end up threatening the health

124

of millions. It was, in fact, nothing short of an environmental disaster.

At the war's end, many hundreds of oil-well fires were spewing toxic smoke and soot that blotted out the sunlight and plunged parts of Kuwait into semidarkness. The smoke was so thick that military officers had to use flashlights to read maps at midday.

"After you breathe it [the air], you start coughing and gagging," said Molly Moore, a correspondent for *The Washington Post*, "and if you look at the windshield of a car, it's all gray, with millions of little black spots on it."

At the same time, enormous oil slicks in the Persian Gulf were killing marine life. No one knew exactly how much oil had been spilled. The Saudi Arabian government estimated the amount to be from 20 million to 120 million gallons. By comparison, the 1989 *Exxon Valdez* spill that devastated Prince William Sound in Alaska was 11 million gallons. Some of the spilled oil was released by the Iraqis to create havoc, and some leaked out of storage facilities, tankers, and wells damaged by the allied bombing.

In addition, large amounts of poisonous chemicals from bombed Iraqi factories and weapon storage areas were released into the atmosphere during the war.

Environmentalists feared the fires could burn for years, filling the sky with sulfurous gases and toxic particles. Crops and water supplies as far away as India could be threatened. Several envi-

Flames and billowing smoke pour from a Kuwaiti oil well torched by Iraqi forces.

ronmental groups called upon the United States and the United Nations to deal with the fires and oil slicks and help organize cleanup efforts.

"The Persian Gulf War may turn out to be the most environmentally destructive conflict in the history of warfare," said Christopher Flavin, a vice-president of the Worldwatch Institute. Michael Renner, a research scientist, called the fires and their toxic gases "an unprecedented atmospheric disaster."

What concerned environmentalists the most were the burning oil wells. When defeat loomed, the Iraqi soldiers attempted to ignite every well in Kuwait. They seemed to have no military reason for creating the disaster. They did it purely out of anger.

They packed the base of each well with enough plastic explosives to destroy an office building, and then detonated them. Of Kuwait's 1,080 high-pressure wells, the Iraqis managed to set 732 ablaze.

The plumes of smoke often shot more than a hundred feet into the air, producing a roar like a jet engine. Temperatures near the fire reached 3,000°, so hot they turned the desert sand to liquid. Within sixty or seventy feet of the fire, the rubber on the soles of shoes would become gummy and start to melt.

At night, the burning well-fires lit the sky with an orange glow. John Pomfret, a reporter for the Associated Press, described the fires as "tornadoes from hell."

In some cases, the explosions destroyed the well-head, the top of the structure built over the well, but failed to ignite the oil. The result was a black geyser that shot into the air. The column of gushing oil created a lake that was several feet deep and kept spreading. Sometimes the pool of oil also burned making it look like the ground itself was on fire. The amount of oil burned in every twenty-four-hour period was equal to the amount of gasoline consumed each day in the United States.

When the war ended, there were few people in Kuwait trained to fight oil-well fires. There was very little firefighting equipment available. Aid had to be brought in from the United States and other countries.

Nearly all of the two- to three-hundred fire-

Workers are shielded from the heat as they attempt to snuff out a burning oil well.

fighters were Texans: machinists, pumping experts, cement experts, and expert welders. Larry Flak, the Houston engineer in charge of putting together the firefighting force stated: "We have explosions experts, heavy machine experts who can make a bulldozer dance, and crane experts who can put a piece of equipment within an inch of its target." The workforce also included six- to seven-hundred support personnel from such countries as India, Pakistan, Egypt, and the Philippines.

Firefighters followed a tried and proven method for putting out the fires. First they would cool the wellhead with high-pressure water hoses as they maneuvered a large crane into position to place an explosive charge above the flames. Once everyone had taken cover, the explosives would be detonated. The explosion would suck all the oxygen away from the fire, smothering it. The crane would then lower a valve unit onto the well. The valves would slowly be closed, stopping the flow of oil. Then, they'd move on to the next well.

As work got underway and the dangerously poisonous smoke continued to billow into the air, the landscape in many parts of Kuwait began to look less and less like the planet Earth. Before the war, the desert sand was dry and powdery. Once the fires began to burn, the desert became covered over with black rain and ash that fell from dark skies.

Kuwait seemed to be under attack from the oil. The smoke and soot irritated the eyes and throat. Many people coughed up black soot. Families with young children who had fled Kuwait during the war were advised not to return until the well fires had been brought under control.

Grazing white sheep turned a dismal gray and they drank from pools of oil-contaminated water. "We eat oil all the time now," said Fatima al-Awadi, a Kuwaiti chemist. "It's in the meat." Toxic chemicals accumulated on much of the nation's farmland, too.

Environmental experts worried about the birds flying through the thick smoke. Some insects were greatly affected. Butterflies were trapped in pools of oil like flies on flypaper. And there were no bees to be seen, although no one knew why.

Environmentalists predicted that the impact of smoke and soot pouring into the air would be felt

A worker from Texas shuts off the valve of a well that had been spewing gas after damage by Iraqi forces.

not only in Kuwait but also in Iran, just to the east, and even as far away as India — in the form of acid rain. Crop damage would certainly result.

The greatest fear from the well fires and the huge clouds of smoke and soot they produced was that they would cause an abrupt change in the climate. In 1982, a group of scientists led by Carl Sagan of Cornell University had concluded that smoke and dust rocketed into the air by a nuclear blast could block out the sunlight. This could plunge parts of the earth into long periods of frigid darkness. The condition came to be called a "nuclear winter."

Some scientists feared that the soot cloud rising over Kuwait could produce something similar. If the wells continued to burn, the world might possibly suffer springtime frosts that would kill crops, and a year without any summer.

By November 1991, the fires were extinguished (and the climate of the region apparently was not affected). But another environmental hazard remained. Some of the wells that had been sabotaged by the Iraqis did not catch fire. Instead, the petroleum poured out of the ground and formed huge oil lakes in the desert. Some of these were more than half a mile wide, more than a mile long, and two to three feet deep.

The oil in the pools seeped into the soil, killing plants and insects. Birds attempting to land on pool surfaces got trapped.

Kuwait hired an army of one hundred fifty foreign and domestic workers to help get rid of the problem. Their plan was to lay pipelines to pump

*An official of the Saudi Arabian government examines
a dead oil-covered cormorant.*

the oil into huge storage tanks. There it would
remain until a way could be found to process it.

In the meantime, the oil in the waters of the
Persian Gulf was creating a catastrophe of its own.
While no one could say exactly how much oil had
poured into the gulf, the spill was known to be
one of the biggest in history.

On January 24, 1991, allied planes bombed two
tankers off of Kuwait, releasing enormous quantities of petroleum. Not long after, Iraqi forces
opened the valves on several pipelines, pouring at
least one hundred thousand barrels of petroleum
a day into the gulf. (One barrel equals forty-two
gallons.) They also opened the pumps on five Kuwaiti tankers carrying 3 million gallons of oil.

President Bush called what the Iraqis did "an

act of environmental terrorism." The Sierra Club said the spills "could destroy the gulf for decades."

The spills wiped out Saudi Arabia's shrimp beds. They devastated sea birds and turtles.

Cleanup efforts involved skimming the oil from the water's surface and pumping it into huge ponds in the desert sand created by bulldozers. One pond was eight feet deep and the size of two football fields. All of the ponds were lined with sheets of plastic.

After only a few weeks, U.S. and Dutch workers had recovered 21 million gallons of oil, about twice the amount spilled by the *Exxon Valdez* into Prince William Sound. The oil would eventually be pumped from the ponds and processed for fuel.

The spilled oil was a tragedy. "Part of the gulf

This shark fell victim to the oil spill off Saudi Arabia's Persian Gulf coast.

could become so saturated with oil that it won't be able to regenerate and support marine life for years," said Robert Skulnik, the executive director of American Oceans Campaign, an environmental group based in Santa Monica, California. "The gulf is a shallow, enclosed ecosystem, and it is possible to pollute to the point of no return."

Other environmentalists were more hopeful. Said Donald R. Leal, a researcher with the Political Economy Research Center, in an article in *The New York Times*: "The oil is relatively light and thus evaporates more quickly than thicker crude. Moreover, the warm waters of the gulf will help marine organisms decompose the oil."

Environmentalists agree, however, that it will be years before the full extent of the damage is known. In the months following the ceasefire, the Persian Gulf War came to look less like a conflict between nations than a war against the planet itself.

What You Can Do

The planet is in trouble. Many of us want to do something about it, but the problems seem enormous. Acid rain. Oil spills. Global warming. Endangered species. No one has the solution to these critical problems.

Yet you *can* help, you *can* make a difference.

To find out what you can do, we have asked some of the nation's foremost environmentalists and government authorities to tell us some starting points. On the pages that follow, they tell how you can contribute toward developing a healthy environment in the years to come.

SENATOR GEORGE J. MITCHELL, MAINE
Majority Leader of Congress

There is a great deal young people can do to help. Letter writing is effective. Young people have a unique perspective on environmental issues that adults simply do not share. They are perhaps the most identifiable victims of environmental degradation. They are hurt most from air and water pollution today and will be forced to live with our toxic waste tomorrow. This makes letters from girls and boys all the more poignant.

I treat mail from young people as special. It does not matter to me if they are from Maine or Montana. Their views are important because the legislation enacted, or not enacted, will directly affect the quality of their life in the future.

Young people can also directly ask members of Congress about environmental issues. No form of communication is more powerful than face-to-face communication. I often visit schools, and, when I do, I am always gratified by the depth of understanding children have about environmental problems. A question from someone in the back row at an assembly can be worth a dozen letters.

Young people can also try to get their parents involved. The more people involved, the greater the chances are for congressional action.

I might also point out that girls and boys can also play an important role at the state and local level. Many important environmental decisions are the province of state and local government. By contacting these officials, young people can have a direct impact on conditions within their own community.

CONSTANCE B. HARRIMAN
Assistant Secretary
for Fish and Wildlife and Parks
U.S. Department of the Interior

What is one thing a young person can do to help save the planet?

Become a local volunteer.

For example, girls and boys, individually and collectively, can:
- start a recycling program for family or school
- begin or participate in park and neighborhood cleanups
- plant trees
- work with civic and community groups to promote a healthy, safe environment

Although the nature of volunteer work may vary between rural and urban areas, the principle of individual action remains the same: Think Globally; Act Locally. Unless our young people cultivate a personal environmental ethic, no amount of government programs can succeed.

GERALD BISHOP
Editor, Ranger Rick
National Wildlife Foundation

Experience nature so thoroughly and so deeply that it becomes a living, breathing part of you — a part of you that you are willing to fiercely defend.

SENATOR JOHN H. CHAFEE, RHODE ISLAND
Ranking Member, Committee on
Environment and Public Works

What steps can young people take to influence public officials to act responsibly on environmental issues?

I believe that involvement at any age in the political process is more than our right as Americans, it is our responsibility. Some might define participation as voting. While voting is certainly critically important to the success of our democratic form of government, it is far from the only means of participating.

While young people are unable to vote, they are able to influence the outcome of elections by volunteering to work on political campaigns of the candidates who are committed to protecting and preserving our environment. This kind of activity has the double benefit of providing the candidate with much-needed assistance and the youngster with grassroots exposure to the political process.

JAY D. HAIR
President, National Wildlife Federation

Today's young people can help save the planet by beginning at an early age to learn as much as they can about their natural environment. This should include learning about their personal impact on local ecosystems as well as their extended impacts on the global environment. Learning about the interdependence among all living things and natural resources empowers a child to become an environmentally responsible citizen. After all, today's young people are tomorrow's "Earth Keepers."

GEORGE T. FRAMPTON, JR.
President, The Wilderness Society

Every young person should try to do something that is naturally very hard for a person who has been alive for only a relatively few years: Try to think in the long term when considering the planet.

The twenty pounds of carbon dioxide that a car spews out while traveling just one mile will go into the atmosphere and affect our climate many years from now. Trees planted today will take decades to become major consumers of carbon. Design decisions made today by those making cars and putting up buildings will be affecting our energy consumption far into the future.

Young people must try to see beyond the next week or next year and try to hand over the planet to future generations in good condition.

PETER A.A. BERLE
President, National Audubon Society

Since the exploration for, and production and use of, fossil fuel energy is the largest contributor to global environment degradation, it is my view that the greatest impact on protecting and restoring our planet could come from greatly increased energy efficiency and the development and use of alternative and renewable energy sources. Young people can educate themselves, their families, and their friends on the many everyday ways they can save energy.

Here is a list of actions people can take to help save energy:

• Walk, bicycle, or use public transportation instead of an automobile whenever possible: Combine errands to make fewer automobile trips.

• Organize car pools.

• Urge your family to buy the most energy-efficient automobiles, thirty miles per gallon or better: Forgo air conditioning in cars.

• Turn off lights when leaving a room.

• Switch from incandescent light bulbs to compact fluorescent bulbs, now available to fit standard lamps and fixtures.

• Decide what you want before opening the refrigerator door, and always close the door quickly.

• Take short showers and install a special water-saving shower head.

• Lower the water-heater control to 120° F.

• Wash dishes by hand, or use a dishwasher only when it is completely full and then set it for an energy-saving cycle.

• Use cool or cold water to wash clothes in a washer. If possible, hang your clothes to dry on a clothline instead of using a dryer.

• Set your home thermostat at 68° F during the winter, and wear sweaters; set it at 80° F during the summer.

Glossary

acid rain — Rain, snow, and other precipitation that has become polluted by chemical compounds given off when coal or oil is burned, when metal ore is smelted, or when gasoline or diesel engines operate.

atmosphere — The body of air surrounding the earth.

biodegradable — Capable of being broken down by natural biological processes such as interaction with bacteria and fungi, into elements such as soil, water, or carbon dioxide.

by-product — Something produced in the making of something else.

carbon dioxide — An odorless, colorless, and tasteless gas. It is produced when gasoline, oil, wood, or any other fuel containing carbon burns with a large supply of oxygen. It is also produced by natural sources such as volcanoes, fires, and the exhaling of humans and animals.

catalytic converter — A device that changes the harmful hydrocarbons a car engine produces into harmless carbon dioxide and water.

decompose — To rot or decay.

ecology — The study of how plants and animals live in relation to one another and their environment.

ecosystem — An ecological community and the species that inhabit it.

emissions — Waste materials discharged into the air, especially by an automobile engine.

endangered — Likely to become an extinct wildlife species, if not protected.

environment — The combination of physical conditions that affect and influence the growth of living things or communities.

Environmental Protection Agency (EPA) — An independent agency of the U.S. government established in 1970 to help protect the nation's environment from pollution. The EPA establishes and enforces environmental standards and conducts research on pollution and its effects.

environmentalist — A person who works to protect the environment.

erosion — The wearing away of soil or rock by wind, water, and other natural processes.

fossil fuel — Fuel such as petroleum, coal, or natural gas, formed from the remains of prehistoric animals.

global warming — The gradual increase in the earth's temperature that some scientists predict will occur because of the greenhouse effect.

greenhouse effect — The behavior of the earth's atmosphere that causes heat from the sun to be trapped near the earth's surface.

groundwater — Water beneath the earth's surface that supplies wells and springs.

habitat — The native environment of an animal or plant.

hazardous wastes — Chemicals and chemical by-products with the potential to endanger human health or pollute the environment.

incinerator — A furnace or other apparatus used for burning trash.

inversion — A condition in which the air temperature increases with altitude, holding surface air — and pollutants — close to the ground.

landfill — A site where garbage and trash are buried beneath a shallow layer of dirt.

nontoxic — Not known to cause injury to humans or wildlife.

ozone — A gas that is formed when nitrogen oxide and hydrocarbons combine in sunlight. In the atmosphere, a thin layer of ozone shields us from the sun's ultraviolet rays. At ground level, however, ozone is a serious health hazard that traps heat and toxic gases.

photovoltaic cell — A device able to generate electric power from the sun's light.

precycle — To buy products made of biodegradable or recyclable materials, thus preventing environmentally harmful materials from entering the waste stream.

rain forest — A dense evergreen forest in a tropical region with an annual rainfall of at least 100 inches.

recycle — To reuse waste materials.

scrubber — An apparatus for removing impurities from smoke or other gases.

solid waste — Garbage and trash not disposed of through a sewer or drain.

species — A group of animals or plants different from all other groups. Members of the group can breed together.

threatened — Likely to become an endangered wildlife species within the foreseeable future.

toxic — Poisonous, hazardous to humans or animal life.

turbine — An engine or a motor which converts the force of water, steam, or air into mechanical power. Turbines are often used to power dynamos that produce electric power.

wetland — A lowland, water-soaked area, such as a swamp or marsh.

Environmental Reading List

Find out more about the environmental topics that interest you through further reading. Useful books include:

The Complete Guide to Recycling at Home by Garry Branson (Better Way Publications).
   How you can do your bit.
Design for a Livable Planet by Jon Naar (HarperCollins).
   Solid advice clearly presented on a wide range of subjects.
The Fate of the Forest: Developers, Destroyers and Defenders of the Amazon by Susanna Hecht and Alexander Cockburn (HarperCollins).
   The struggle of destroyers and defenders over the future of a vast and precious ecological area.
50 Simple Things Kids Can Do to Save the Earth by the Earthworks Group (Andres and McNeel).
   Lively, fun-to-read tips.
The Green Consumer Supermarket Guide by John Makower (Penguin Books).
   Consumer tips for a healthy planet.

Hawk, I'm Your Brother by Byrd Baylor (Macmillan).
A boy who wants to fly like a bird captures a hawk and then sets it free. In so doing, he comes to understand the relation between humans and animals.

The Kids' Environment Book: What's Awry and Why by Anne Pedersen (John Muir Publications).
Discussion of environmental problems.

The Lorax by Dr. Seuss (Random House).
What happens when, through greediness, we use up our natural resources.

1001 Ways to Save the Planet by Bernadette Vallely (Ivy/Ballantine).
Saving the environment, one step at a time.

The Rainforest Book by Scott Lewis (Living Planet Press).
What you can do to help preserve the world's rain forests.

Save the Animals, 101 Easy Things You Can Do by Ingrid Newkirk (Warner Books).
Bright ideas and practical suggestions.

The Wump World by Bill Peet (Houghton Mifflin).
An invasion by the Pollutians, who turn the green meadows into a concrete jungle.

Index

Page references in italics indicate material in illustrations.